Ready? Set? Go!

Also by Judy Hampton

Under the Circumstances: A Woman's Guide to a Surrendered Heart

Ready? Set? Go!

How Parents of Prodigals Can Get On With Their Lives

Judy Hampton

Ready? Set? Go!: How Parents of Prodigals Can Get On With Their Lives

Biblical references are taken from *THE MESSAGE: The Bible in Contemporary Language,* © 2002 Eugene Peterson, NavPress; *The Zondervan NASB Study Bible,* © 1999 the Zondervan Corporation; *The Life Application Bible: The New International Version,* published jointly by Tyndale House Publishers, Inc. and Zondervan Publishing House, © 1973, 1978, 1984; and *New King James Version,* © 1979, 1980, 1982 Thomas Nelson, Inc.

Published by Hats Off Books®
610 East Delano Street, Suite 104
Tucson, Arizona 85705 U.S.A.
www.hatsoffbooks.com

International Standard Book Number: 1-58736-472-7
Library of Congress Control Number: 2005923354

This book is gratefully dedicated to
Sue Burchett
Sue and I have suffered and rejoiced together with
prodigals. Her faithful friendship is unparalleled.
Sue and her husband experienced the joy of seeing their
prodigal come back to the Lord.

This book is also in
loving memory of Sue's husband
Steven N. Burchett
Steve went home to be with His Heavenly Father
March 5, 2004

Contents

My friend, I don't know what you're going through, but look and see if God is trying to direct you, inspect you, correct you, protect you, or perfect you.

Anonymous

Ready? Set? Go!

Prologue

PERHAPS YOU HAVE picked up this book because you are the parent of a prodigal child, and you've put your life on hold. Maybe your heart is broken, leaving you in a state of despair and suffering. You find it hard to go on with your life. You've tried everything to help and nothing changes. You've run out of answers. You've even lost hope for a normal future. Maybe you are weary of the gut-wrenching pain. Possibly you feel some guilt and blame yourself for your prodigal's choices. In turn, your prodigal blames you! You can't change the past and the future is out of your hands, too. Would it make you feel a little bit better knowing you are part of an epidemic that is sweeping our country? Parents with Prodigals!

In the Scripture a prodigal is referred to as someone who has walked away from God. Someone who is living apart from God, or has exchanged living for Him, for living for self. Sometimes prodigals are openly rebellious. Others are just passively indifferent to the things of God.

I feel like an expert on prodigals. I know what it is like to be one, and to have had one.

Looking back at my teenage years, I know I hurt my parents deeply. I thought little of them at the time. I was the center of my universe. When I was seventeen, I broke my mother's heart when I told her I was pregnant. She said I'd ruined *her* life! She was embarrassed and ashamed of me. My pregnancy disgraced our family.

Later, after I was married, I never considered Mom's feelings when I dumped all my marriage problems in her lap. But neither Mom nor Dad ever rescued me from my problems.

I blamed my dad the most. Blame eased my guilt. Dad struggled with alcoholism and unemployment in my teenage years. I became the rescuing, responsible child/parent. I worked after school, fended for myself, and gave a lot of my paychecks to my dad to make ends meet. But Dad abandoned our family on my graduation day. He left behind a suicide note. Devastated, I fell into temptation and ended up in the arms of my high school sweetheart and ... well, you know the rest!

Daddy eventually came home from a binge. I was grateful beyond words he didn't take his life, but deep inside I blamed him for all my lost dreams. Daddy never asked forgiveness for the pain he put our family through.

Reflecting on my early years as a parent, I feel tons of guilt over my role as a mother. I loved my children so much, but I was so young, extremely self-centered, and the stress of poverty strained our marriage to the breaking point. I *could* blame my behavior on my family of origin, Dad's alcoholism, my immaturity, selfishness, poverty, and bleak circumstances. But the truth is, I am a sinner.

I came to saving faith in Jesus Christ after eight tumultuous years of marriage. An immediate paradigm shift took place! I was a new creation in Christ. I was forgiven for all my sins … past, present, and future. What unspeakable joy when my husband gave his life to Christ three months later. We experienced the miracle of watching God slowly resurrect our dead marriage from the graveyard. However, because of my shallow faith and naiveté, I thought now we would be the perfect Christian family, and live happily ever after.

Imagine our surprise years later when we found ourselves the parents of a prodigal.

"This can't be! Our child is a Christian. And we're Christians! Aren't Christians supposed to be immune from this?" I questioned.

Paralyzed with disbelief, we did what most parents do. We tried to fix things. We tried to make our prodigal's life better. We tried rescuing and enabling. It went on for years. Why? I, for one, was an expert at it. I'd learned from an early age how to *try* to fix a person, even though it never really worked. But my husband and I sincerely wanted to help. And we wanted the pain to end. Admittedly, it eased some of the regret over our early years of parenting.

As time passed, however, we found ourselves jeopardizing our financial future to dig our prodigal out of one hole after another. We bought cars, fixed cars, paid for insurance, cosigned for loans, lent money, paid traffic tickets, and paid for counseling. We believed the litany of excuses. The revolving door to our "rent free" house appeared to spin out of control. But nothing changed long term.

"What do we do, when all we've done is just not enough?" we asked ourselves on a regular basis. The turmoil put a lot of strain on our marriage.

We questioned God. "Why is this happening? Where did we go wrong? Are we being punished for our own sin? God, we stayed together, we didn't get a divorce, we worked out our own problems and taught our children about You. We really tried to make up for our past mistakes. How can a child who was so loved, so applauded for every achievement, spent years in a thriving, evangelical church make such a mess out of life? What do we do now? We can't rewrite the past, as much as we'd like to, and the future seems hopeless."

I confess we were mortified that friends would find out about our family. Christians didn't talk about their problems then. What would people think? We feared our non-Christian friends would learn of our hidden heartache, especially since their children seemed to be doing so well. We didn't want them to question our God.

Like running through a maze, we searched for a way out. "Help us! Help us!" we pleaded as we ran everywhere looking for help and advice. But we kept running into dead ends. Disillusioned, we discovered the futility of man's wisdom, ideologies, theories, and behavior modification. It only provided us with temporary relief, but no lasting peace *or* change.

We were living a nightmare, the kind where you are trying desperately to run away from someone chasing you, but your feet are stuck in a rubbery muck. We were *consumed* with our prodigal. We had no idea we were in the biggest spiritual battle of our lives.

When we ran out of options, we hit the wall, so to speak. With no place to turn, we finally turned to God. It's rather embarrassing how long it took us to do this. Yet God, out of His mercy and grace, met us right where we were.

The purpose of this book

This book is written to help parents of adult prodigals get on with their lives, with practical steps for parents who are stuck trying to cope. It's a book to help parents grant themselves permission to let go of their prodigals, and give them to God.

Hurting parent, I want to assure you there is abundant life beyond a prodigal. You must ask yourself, "Am I ready to find it? Do I really want to break free from the stranglehold my prodigal has on my heart? Do I want to learn a new way of living?" If you are ready, I can assure you that God is waiting to give you new life, and mend your broken heart. But you must give Him *all* the pieces.

Getting on with your life is not something you can conjure up through your own power. We can put no confidence in our flesh. Finding a new way of living is dependent on God's strength. It is *not* about self-help, positive thinking, or mind control. It's a gift only God can provide from *within*. In fact, it's the reality of the Christian life. Peace in the midst of pain! Are you ready? Set? Then let's go!

Chapter One

The Pathway of a Prodigal

I RECENTLY READ this item in *Christian Parenting Today* magazine:

"While listening to the song 'Train Up a Child,' my daughter Emily asked me, 'What does train up mean?'

"I explained that it means to teach children about God and the difference between right and wrong.

"'Are you and Daddy training me up?' she asked.

"'We're trying to,' I said.

"Emily turned back to the stereo and muttered, 'We'll see about that.'"

That's a cute story, but it is also an eye-opening truth for parents. No matter how dedicated we are as parents, we are still raising a child who has a will of their own. Some stronger than others. Admittedly, there were times I wanted to "chain up my child," because I did *not* have control.

Parents can have great and grandiose plans for raising their children and teaching them right from wrong. However, eventually those children will grow into adolescents and then adults. They will be alone with their choices and decisions at one point or another.

Unfortunately, a parent cannot make those choices for them.

The parable of the prodigal son is the most familiar and beloved of all Christ's parables. It is one of the longest and most detailed parables. It's about choices. It also has more than one lesson.

The first lesson is that all people come into this world separated from God because of their sin (Isaiah 59:1–2). Yet this parable speaks of God's love and eagerness to restore us to Himself and forgive us.

The second lesson is about two sons. Two kinds of prodigals. The younger son goes out and *openly* sins, eventually repents, and comes home to the father. The older son lives the principled, religious life. He doesn't do culturally bad things. He looks really good on the outside. But in his heart he is self-righteous, prejudiced, indifferent to repentant sinners, and spiritually *dead.* He himself *is* an unrepentant sinner, but he sees himself through prideful eyes. He's just counting on his good works for salvation, not God's finished work (Titus 3:4–5).

Whether you are struggling with an openly rebellious child or one who is passively indifferent to spiritual things, both are living independently from God.

The story of the prodigal son is found in the Book of Luke, Chapter 15, beginning with verse 11.

The younger son decides he'd like to leave home and see if the grass in really greener on the other side of the fence. His flesh is centered on gratifying himself and running his own life. However, to do this he needs some financing. So he goes to his dad and asks for an early inheritance. The truth is, this son is making a very unreasonable request. Why? He is putting his dad in a tight spot financially, not to mention the fact he is also breaking his dad's heart. Under Jewish law, the *oldest* son would receive two-thirds of the inheritance. The rest would go to the younger son upon the death of the father. This request is tantamount to saying he wishes his father were dead. But, like most prodigals, he is not thinking about his dad, or anyone else. He is only thinking about himself. And, like most parents, the father loves his son, and wants to make him happy. So he gives him the money.

Most parents I meet give money to their children out of pure motives and great love. What parent doesn't want to help their children?

However, the prodigal son takes the money, all his possessions, and leaves. He has no plans for returning home. He goes far away and lives a dissolute lifestyle. He probably goes far away so no one he knows will see him, especially his father. He is planning on doing things that are wrong. Imagine what it's like when he rolls into town with his pockets full of money. He probably makes some friends fast! So, they take advantage of him, and they live it up! The wild life! Not merely wasteful extravagance, but wanton immorality.

It should be pointed out that the prodigal didn't live in a terrible home. In fact, it seems like a very stable home. There is no account of any abuse. No divorce. No blended family. No stepparents. No alcoholism. No financial strain. No abandonment. This home was filled with love, and the love of his father. This young man had everything he could possibly want, from a roof over his head to fine clothes. This home even had servants. There was also faith in this home. Maybe the father read the Scriptures to his family. But the son still wanted to leave and live it up!

God was the perfect father

We must remember that God, the Perfect Father, watched His first two *perfect* children, Adam and Eve, fall into sin (Genesis 2 and 3). Imagine their life up until they were deceived. They had it all! They lived in paradise. All their needs were met ... and they enjoyed God's presence daily. They had no blended family, no stepparents, no children, no pressure on the job, no stress, no floods, no droughts, no irreconcilable differences, and no peer pressure. They didn't even have in-laws!

God told them to enjoy everything He'd given them, with one exception. "Don't eat from the tree in the middle of the garden. That is the tree of the knowledge of good and evil. If you eat from it you will die" (Gen. 3:3).

Well, that must have been one *no* too many. They were given a choice and didn't want any restraints. They wanted to be their own god. So they listened to the enemy twist God's Word, and with two bites, sin entered into this world.

God knew what they had done because He is omnipresent. They even tried to hide from Him. Prodigals *always* try to hide from God.

Well, what they did next was classic victimization. They began to blame someone else for their sin. Sound familiar? Eve blamed the serpent and Adam blamed Eve. But it didn't wash with God. He instituted tough love and grave consequences. He not only banished them from paradise, but He gave them a life sentence of hard work and pain. From that moment on, they were separated from God. Their very first child became a murderer!

You know the story of how Adam landed us in the dilemma we're in ... first sin, then death, and no one is exempt from either sin or death. That sin disturbed relations with God in everything and everyone, but the extent of the disturbance was not clear until God spelled it out in detail to Moses. So death, this huge abyss separating us from God, dominated the landscape from Adam to Moses. Even those who didn't sin precisely as Adam did by disobeying a specific command of God still had to experience this termination of life, this separation from God (Romans 5:12–14, *The Message*).

The Scripture shows me that we are all born prodigals: "All have sinned and fallen short of the glory of God" (Romans 3:23). Scripture tells me that there are no perfect parents. No guarantees. Many of the most godly people in Scripture had rebellious children. Many rebellious parents in Scripture had godly children. Due to the uncertainty of life and the unpredictable behavior of fallen man, no parent can determine the outcome of their children.

Here's a story from a man who admits he grew up in a wonderful home, yet made sinful choices.

"I was raised in what everyone would think was a perfect home. My parents were Christians and pillars of the church. When I reached puberty, like every other boy I was interested in sex. My parents weren't very good at sharing at an intimate level, so most of what I learned about sex was from my friends and a book my parents had in the house. From the book I learned how to masturbate and I became a slave to it. I was in my own private world. On the outside I was this Christian kid, involved with the youth group, a counselor at a Christian camp, and a member of the 'perfect family.' On the inside I was in complete bondage to pornography and lustful thinking.

I went to a Christian college and married a lovely Christian girl, and we were the 'perfect couple.' But I still had this private world that my wife didn't even know about. My addiction continued to get worse since I was on the road a lot with my job. Of course it finally happened (adultery) again and again. I knew it was wrong, but I couldn't stop. I would have guilt and remorse, but no true repentance."

The story goes on to say that when he came to the end of himself, repented, and sought the Lord's power to change him, he was set free. His parents did not accomplish this *for* him.

I know God delights in restoring repentant sinners and giving them a new life. He wants to restore your prodigal. But prodigals must come to the end of themselves and turn to God for help and restoration.

Steps to getting on with your life

- ✣ Realize we are *all* born into this world with a sinful nature, and a will of our own.
- ✣ God allows us to make choices.
- ✣ Stop blaming yourself for being a less-than-ideal parent and having a prodigal.
- ✣ We see from the Scripture that God was the perfect parent, and look what happened to both of His children.
- ✣ The prodigal son's father appears to have been a very good parent, and look what happened to both of his children.

✳ There is no such thing as a perfect parent. Even the very best have been known to have rebellious children. Because of the uncertainty of life, we cannot predict the behavior of fallen humanity.

✳ God loves your prodigal more than you do. But you cannot make your prodigal change.

✳ Would you be willing to leave your prodigal in God's hands?

✳ Would you be willing to participate in the plan God has for *your* life (Jeremiah 29:11)?

✳ Getting on with your life requires God's supernatural strength, not determination (Psalm 28:7).

"You are not primarily a product of your past, you are primarily a product of the work of Christ on the cross and His resurrection. Your beliefs determine how you live."

—Neil Anderson

Chapter Two

When Your World Falls Apart

"No man knows what a day may bring forth."
—Proverbs 27:1

MY PHONE RANG very late at night. I heard my friend Debbie's frantic cries on my answering machine. I picked up the receiver, and prepared myself for the continuing saga of the heartache of living with a prodigal child.

Debbie, like all hurting parents, was *consumed* with her daughter. She had good reason. Her daughter was pregnant, and her teenage boyfriend was a deadbeat on drugs. I'd heard her story over and over again. I listened patiently. Debbie was frantic for answers. She wanted *someone* to help her and tell her how she could fix the whole mess.

"Judy, I don't know what to do! Tell me what to do. I feel like I am at the end of my rope over this mess. My husband and I are at odds, and he won't allow her to reap any consequences. He's afraid she'll be out on the streets if we don't take care of her. And who knows? He may be right. So he wants her to live at *our* home *with* this ghastly boyfriend until the baby is born, so they can save money to get married. Just the thought of them marrying gives me the shivers. Her boyfriend doesn't even work.

"Oh Judy, I can't imagine this! She's verbally abusive to us and she and her boyfriend fight *all* the time. She's so self-consumed! I can't believe she is even part of our family. She doesn't give another thought to anyone else but herself! I know she's probably into drugs as well, and I don't know what to do. Judy, I need some help."

My friend's world had fallen apart. She was in a downward spiral. She was so embarrassed people would find out about their daughter. She just wanted someone to lend her some hope.

One source of hope is friends who help bear your burdens. It reminds me of a poem I read years ago.

Lend Me Your Hope

Lend me your hope for awhile, I seem to have mislaid mine.

Lost and hopeless feelings accompany me daily, pain and confusion are my companions.

I know not where to turn; looking ahead to future times does not bring forth images of renewed hope.

I see troubled times, pain-filled days, and more tragedy.

Lend me your hope for awhile, I seem to have mislaid mine.

Hold my hand and hug me; listen to all my ramblings, recovery seems so far distant.

The road to healing seems like a long and lonely one.

Lend me your hope for awhile, I seem to have mislaid mine.

Stand by me, offer me your presence, your heart and your love.

Acknowledge my pain, it is so real and ever present.

I am overwhelmed with sad and conflicting thoughts.

Lend me your hope for awhile; a time will come when I will heal, and I will share my renewal, hope, and love with others.

(Author unknown)

I tried to lend my friend some hope and encouragement. When grief is the freshest, words should be the fewest. I was there to listen and love. I acknowledged her pain and her deep disappointment.

But in time, friends must encourage their discouraged friends to take the hand of God. That's my goal in this book. You need supernatural power to make it through this trial.

"May the God of hope fill you with all joy and peace in believing, that you may abound in hope by the power of the Holy Spirit" (Romans 15:13).

When Our World Fell Apart

I'll never forget how our lives changed in twenty-four hours.

We'd just finished a nice dinner, but before I could clear the table my husband put his hand on my arm and asked me to wait a minute.

"Honey, I have something I have to tell you," he said in a morose tone of voice.

I felt a flip-flop in my stomach. I just knew it was bad news. Like waiting for a diagnosis from the doctor.

"I got a call two days ago. It's not good. I didn't know how in the world to break the news to you, so I put it off until now. Um ... Judy ... we cannot see our grandchildren any more."

Now I felt a sensation in my stomach you feel when you've been kicked. Like the oxygen had been removed from my lungs. I sensed I would collapse. A wave of nausea and even lightheadedness followed.

"I don't get it. What's wrong?" I said, almost cotton-mouthed.

"We've been accused of being terrible parents, and I was told we would no longer be given the opportunity to have that kind of influence on our grandchildren."

Fact and truth took over my refusal to understand. Now I felt we'd been victims of a hit-and-run accident.

Crushed emotionally, I took a deep breath and then started sobbing.

"What are you talking about? This makes no sense! We've never done anything but lavish our love and attention on our grandchildren. Why would parents punish their innocent little children because they are struggling with their marriage, and other problems? Why are we being dragged into this? What are we going to do? What are the grandchildren going to think when suddenly we are no longer in their lives? They will be heartbroken! Oh God, please don't let this be happening. I can't live without them," I said as I rambled into a whisper, out of breath.

Our world fell apart many years ago. Up until that time, it was as though we'd lived through an endless roller-coaster ride of trauma and drama with our prodigal.

But this time was different. Innocent children were being punished along with us! A forest fire had been set, and we were the fire. The smoke from the fire was to camouflage the *real* problem. Our prodigal's problem!

Life lessons in the midst of a firestorm

As we began to break through this raging firestorm, we learned some critical life lessons. I want to share them with you throughout this book, so that you will take comfort in knowing you are not alone.

Adversity is the pits. It's difficult. It usually takes us by surprise and seems to strike where we are most vulnerable. For most parents, it's their children or grandchildren. It seems senseless and irrational, but to God none of it is. Jerry Bridges put it this way: "We discovered that God is never the author of sin. Though people's sinful intents and actions are used *by* Him to serve His sovereign purposes."

Pain and unthinkable circumstances are great teachers. Oh, some are brutal to be sure, but it's really the only time we seem to learn and grow spiritually. God has to teach us that every adversity that comes across our path, whether large or small, is intended to help us grow in some area of our life.

Solomon said, "When times are good, be happy; but when times are bad, consider: God has made the one as well as the other" (Ecclesiastes 7:14).

Steps to getting on with your life

✱ Hurting parent, friends can be there to help shoulder your burdens. But supernatural, transforming power and peace come only from God and His Word. Cry out to Him for help.

* The abundant life we are *all* searching for is found when we are centered on God, not our problems.
* If God is going to use you and me, He will bring adversity into our lives so that we, too, may learn experientially to depend on Him. Learning this is not a five-minute task we check off our Palm Pilot. *It's a process* that takes some time. You and I are not a finished work (Phil.1:6).
* During this process you will discover that Jesus is right there with you. When you need Him the most, He is there. He is nearest to the broken-hearted.
* As bad as things seem, I promise you they will become good things in the hands of God.
* Realize that this time in your life is part of your story and what makes you uniquely you.

"As sure as God ever puts His children into the furnace, He will be in the furnace with them."
—Charles Haddon Spurgeon

Chapter Three

Why Did This Happen?

"Pain is the gift nobody wants, but it's a gift from God."
—Phillip Yancy

ONE OF MY dearest friends had a goal to be the perfect mother. Donna was a stay-at-home mom and loved every single thing about it. She made her two daughters the focus of her life, as did her husband.

She took them to all their lessons—ballet, piano, voice, gymnastics—and to endless soccer practices and games. She and her husband never missed a thing their girls were involved in, and they were their biggest cheerleaders.

Donna lavishly decorated her home for every holiday, creating precious memories for her girls. She allowed them to decorate their bedrooms in whatever theme they wanted, and she bought them the latest style of clothes. Donna left little off their Christmas wish list. Birthdays were *always* a big event. Grandparents, aunts, uncles, and cousins always gathered for the celebrations. Each summer they took a wonderful family vacation to a lakefront resort. Their family times were precious.

Donna and her husband made sure the girls were in Sunday school and church every week. She prayed with them before they went to bed, and talked to them on a regular basis about God. They were taught the Bible and memorized Scriptures! Donna and her husband took the time to clearly present the Gospel to them. They explained how Jesus was crucified on a cross to pay for sin. He died, He was buried, and three days later He arose from the grave. They knew Jesus conquered death to give them eternal life. Donna's children knew that if they asked Jesus Christ to forgive them their sins, and received Him as their Lord and Savior, they would become a part of the family of God and live forever with Him in heaven.

Donna's older daughter, Melody, followed all the rules. She seemed like the perfect daughter in every way. She was obedient, diligent in her schoolwork, popular, a cheerleader, and involved in youth groups and missions.

Their younger daughter, Barbara, seemed to be following the same path. She and her older sister made Donna proud to be their Mom.

But then something happened! When Barbara was in the seventh grade, it was as if someone flipped a switch in her heart.

"She went from being a precious daughter to a little demon," Donna said. "She started having problems in school, and was put in a class for incorrigible children. She actually loved it because she could relate to the rest of the rebellious kids. 'Birds of a feather ...' Life at home became a constant battlefield. Barbara knew she had other choices to make but she decided to go her own way and blatantly disobey us."

Donna and her husband fell into despair as they helplessly watched their once lovely daughter walk away from everything she knew was right.

By the time Barbara was in the eighth grade, Donna decided to enroll her in a Christian school. She hoped the spiritual environment would help turn her heart back to God. But in three short months she was kicked out because of insubordination. She broke all the rules! She was bent on doing whatever she wanted, and didn't care who she hurt.

"Barbara was *always* on restriction. But it was a joke. She would sneak out of the house in the middle of the night, and take her dad's car. Then she would party the night away, drinking, smoking, and who knows what else! She got two citations for driving under the influence of alcohol. She was taken down to the police station, and of course the police called us! Our daughter was in jail! It was the worst experience of our life!"

Why us? Why this?

For nine painful years Donna and her husband questioned God. "Why us? Why this? Where did we go wrong?" They simply couldn't make sense of this trial.

They watched their once lovely daughter change before their eyes. Where once she enjoyed the company of her Barbie dolls and pretty clothes, now she hung out with people who looked like convicts. She distanced herself from everything she had been taught. Her blatant disrespect was hurled at everyone, even her grandparents. She did not care how much her words hurt.

"I was a mess throughout the whole ordeal," Donna said. "Gripped with fear nearly twenty-four hours a day, I did everything I could to save our daughter. Then the unthinkable happened! She got pregnant at seventeen! I was livid and hysterical at the same time! All the dreams I had for her were gone. I wanted her to go to college, meet and marry a nice Christian man, and have 'perfect children.' God, what happened to my dreams and plans?

"We decided to allow her to continue to live with us throughout the pregnancy and after the baby arrived. We wanted to give our grandchild a stable and loving home because Barbara refused to turn from her life of sin. She wasn't interested in her baby at all.

"But one day, when least expected, Barbara woke up and came to her senses. She found that the pigpen she was living in stunk! The pleasure of sin grew less and less satisfying. She was tired of her life.

"Easter rolled around and she agreed to attend an Easter service with us at a church right down the street from our home. We had never attended there before. The pastor gave the beautiful message of salvation by grace and the Holy Spirit spoke to our daughter's heart. After the sermon was over, imagine how shocked we were when our daughter walked to the altar and gave her life to Jesus Christ! We wanted to rejoice, but we were cautious to see if it was genuine.

"Immediately we saw Barbara's life dramatically change. She stopped hanging out with her old friends, and began studying her Bible. She began praying for God's direction and His will for her life.

"What was God teaching us? First of all, this trial revealed how shallow our faith was. How dependent it was on our daughter and happy happenings. How deceived we'd been. Thinking we could determine the outcome of another person's life and then practically worship that person. God showed us that we worried more about what people thought of us, but never considered what He thought of us. Our daughter's rebellion turned out to be a gift from God.

"Barbara encouraged us to start getting into God's Word and seeking His will and direction for our lives. It was a pivotal point in our spiritual maturing process.

"In a few years Barbara met and married a wonderful Christian man. He had a rebellious past, too, and had fathered a child out of wedlock," Donna said, crying. "No one would believe the miracle of their lives."

Donna would probably say she wouldn't take a million dollars for her experience. But you couldn't pay her five million dollars to go through it again! Yet God used this trial to change a mom and a dad and a whole family. He is still using their story to minister to other hurting, discouraged parents.

When I read the Scriptures I see that other parents have struggled with their children. Yet I am encouraged to see that God used these men for His purpose and to bring glory to Himself. These stories have encouraged hurting parents for centuries to trust God! Here's an example of two men, Samson and Manasseh.

Samson had such incredible potential. He was raised in a very godly home. But he messed up, and made more than his share of poor choices. Like all of us, he became deceived. Deceived by the world, the flesh, and the devil. Yet, *in spite of* all his sin and poor choices, God used him to free Israel from Philistine oppression.

Hezekiah was a man of God and a great king. He did what was right in the sight of the Lord. When his son Manasseh became king, he did more *evil* in the sight of the

Lord than *any other king* did. Detestable practices! Sacrificed his sons in the fire! Practiced sorcery, divination, witchcraft, and consulted with mediums and psychics. Like the prodigal son, Manasseh was far from God, and he did not look like someone who *ever* knew right from wrong. These actions made God extremely angry.

But here is the great news! When Manasseh came to his senses, he sought the Lord. He repented and turned away from his sin and cried out to God in humility. He prayed, and the Lord listened and helped him. He finally realized the Lord alone is God! So God restored Manasseh and forgave all the sins of his youth.

Then Manasseh went on to tear down all the idols and restored the temple and encouraged the people to seek the Lord. Manasseh started outdoing evil and ended up strong for the Lord. This story should really encourage parents with prodigals. God is doing a work in you and your prodigal.

"If you look at your problem and then look at God, you always end up throwing stones at God for the problem," wrote Dr. Joseph Stowell. "If you look at God first and look at your problems through Him, through His sovereignty, and that He is in control of everything, that He has permitted this in your life for a reason, that He is a just God, that He will settle the score for you, you will see that He is an all-powerful God who can turn this situation to that which is good and right."

Steps to getting on with your life

❉ Parent, can you imagine this time with your prodigal could be a gift? If you are wondering why you are going through this pain, please understand that

God has allowed it. He allows *every* trial (Job 42:2, Psalms 115:3, Psalms 119:75, Isaiah 14:27, Isaiah 43:13, Isaiah 46:10, Daniel 4:35 and Ephesians 1:11).

* When we ask why, it's because we have a wrong view of God. But He cares more than we'll ever know.

* All trials have spiritual significance. They are not obstacles, they are opportunities! God is refining you and building your character. He is also working in your prodigal's life, even though you may not see it.

* Look at your problem through God first. God promises He'll work everything you are going through for the good (Romans 8:28). Donna never dreamed how God would change her daughter, and of the work He did in their family. Donna has been used by God to encourage many hurting parents.

"Faith is believing in things when common sense tells you not to."

—George Seaton

Chapter Four

We're in a War,
but It's Winnable

"We will lose a battle or two, but not the war."
—Spiros Zodhiates

I MET A woman a few years ago at a retreat. She was having an emotional meltdown over her son's rebellion.

In the course of our conversation, I couldn't help but notice how lovely she was. She wore designer clothes, had exquisite platinum jewelry, her hair was perfectly highlighted, she had perfect nails, and looked faultless! As we spoke more about her life, I learned her husband had a thriving business and they owned several homes throughout the country. It seemed to me their son was standing in the way of their otherwise perfect life.

I asked her about his problem and she gave me a socially accepted diagnosis from a physician. It makes it easier than admitting you have a child who is a drug addict.

"He can't help it! He's addicted to drugs because of this disorder. We've spent over $100,000 on in-patient treatment through a famous university hospital program with the highest reputation in the country! Now he's back on drugs again. He only stayed sober as long as he was part of the in-patient treatment," she snapped.

"Now I'm so frustrated because we are going to have to shell out another $100,000 to get him clean and sober again. The biggest problem is he hates the medication he must take. He says he can't have sex when he's taking it! So he goes off his pills and then falls back into his addiction."

I swallowed, rather wide-eyed.

"I'm really sorry. I can tell your heart is broken. May I ask how old is your son?"

"He's twenty-two."

"Have you ever thought of trying something different? Your see, your son is an adult. Maybe he really doesn't want to change. Many people with addictions know they have a problem, but they don't *really* want to give it up! Have you thought of letting him live on his own? This might force him to reap the consequences of his choices."

My body tightened as I braced myself for her response.

"Oh, God! We couldn't do that!" she shrieked. "What in the world would people think of us if we stopped taking care of our son? I told you, he can't help it. Besides, my husband's reputation is at stake. How could we risk that? Jesus told us to love others unconditionally. How would letting him go out on his own be loving? What if he got hurt? What if he ended up in the gutter? What if he died?" she asked as she started to cry.

"No doubt this is a difficult dilemma. But this is a time to put your trust in God. And I think we can love our children unconditionally without financing their rebellious lifestyle or rewarding them for it," I reasoned.

As I spoke, gals in her Bible study group stood behind her, giving me the thumbs-up sign. It seems everyone, including her pastor, had given her similar counsel!

God's love is often tough

I have found that there is a real tension in the Scripture about love, tough love, and discipline.

God's Word assures us that He never stops *loving* us. Yet His love is often tough when we are out of fellowship because of our sin. Then He loves us from afar.

The writer of Hebrews said this: "My son, do not make light of the Lord's discipline, and do not lose heart when he rebukes you, because the Lord disciplines those he loves, and he punishes everyone he accepts as a son" (Hebrews 12:5–6).

"But don't, dear friend, resent God's discipline; don't sulk under his loving correction. It's the child he loves that God corrects; a father's delight is behind all this" (Proverbs 3:11–12).

As we revisit the parable of the prodigal son, we do not read that the father ever chased after his son. He didn't try to change his mind or think about it a while. He gave him his money and I believe he gave him to God. He knew God would work.

We are not being unloving if we separate ourselves from our prodigal! Separating protects love, because we are taking a stand against the things that destroy love.

In the next chapter we will discover the power that the pigpen had on the prodigal son. It has the same power today.

The principles of warfare

I think it is critical to understand that the battle parents face with a prodigal has more than one dimension. There is a third party involved. His name is Satan.

Throughout the New Testament (with a concentration of teaching in Ephesians) God reminds us that *we are in a conflict*. The conflict you are in with your prodigal is not simply with flesh and blood. It is also a spiritual conflict, with principals and powers and spiritual wickedness in high places. It's essential to know the tactics of the enemy so you won't be caught off guard. If you don't recognize your enemy for what he is and if you aren't aware of his tricks and devices, it makes it easier for him to push his way into your life until he holds you captive through *fear*. Gripping, paralyzing fear. The kind that keeps you awake at night, and unable to concentrate during the day. Unable to get on with your life.

I have learned that we need to be trained to become warriors through the Lord Jesus Christ. We cannot ignore warfare principles and expect to win battles. We can stand against Satan (Ephesians 6:11) because the victory has been won. "Thanks be to God who gives us the victory through our Lord Jesus Christ" (I Corinthians 15:57).

Remember, children who are rebellious living apart from God's will are under the influence of evil as well. In the Old Testament rebellion was referred to as the sin of witchcraft (I Samuel 15:23).

The first symptom of the spiritual battle in prodigals is obvious: a loss of interest in spiritual things. Their sin has broken fellowship with God, and the Holy Spirit makes them uncomfortable. This isn't always outward. Sometimes it is simply passive indifference to the things of God. Other symptoms may be arrogance, blame, victimization, lying, verbal abuse, deceitfulness, and even blatant rage, to name but a few. Parent, have you ever tried to *reason* with a rebellious child? Remember Donna's daughter Barbara? They could not reason with her, and felt someone had flipped a switch in her heart. That switch was flipped by the evil one. Satan gets no greater unholy pleasure than ruining people's lives.

For the parent, a sense of hopelessness, discouragement, and even a lack of faith in God can take place. The way to avoid the vulnerability of these emotions is to focus on what you *know* to be true about God, not on the question marks of what you *don't* know about your problem. Satan is a great distracter. He doesn't want you to trust God with anything, he wants you to trust your emotions!

Back to basics

When we are saved we are filled with the Holy Spirit, and we cannot lose our salvation because we are saved by grace (Ephesians 2:8). However, we can stifle the Holy Spirit's flow when we are disobedient or living in sin, and are out of fellowship with God (2 John 1:8). Restoration only comes when we confess our sin, repent, and turn back to God.

Positionally, Satan's power over Christians is already broken and the great war is won through Christ's crucifixion and resurrection, which forever conquered the power of sin and death (Romans 5:18–21, I Corinthians 15:56–57, Hebrews 2:14).

However, in life on earth, battles of temptation go on regularly. Daily! The Lord's power through the strength of His Spirit (Luke 10:19, 20) and the force of biblical truth is required for victory. "For though we walk in the flesh, we do not war according to the flesh. For the weapons of our warfare are not of the flesh, but divinely powerful for the destruction of fortresses" (2 Corinthians 10:3–4).

What the Apostle Paul is saying here is that we walk in the flesh in a physical sense, but we cannot fight spiritual battles by using human ingenuity. Those weapons are *useless* to free souls from the forces of darkness. Only *spiritual* weapons can demolish spiritual strongholds. Weapons yielded by believers.

Christ Himself referred to Satan as the prince of this world system (John 12:31 and 16:11). He is not equal to the Most High God, but we can only walk in the victory Christ won for us when we are "strong in the Lord and in his mighty power" (Ephesians 6:10). "Greater is He Who is in us, than he who is in the world" (I John 4:4). Satan is not more powerful than God.

Where the battle begins

So where does this battle begin? It begins in the mind. Never forget this principle, for understanding it is the key to winning the war. The way we think determines the way we live (Proverbs 23:7a). At any moment, if we are experiencing *anything* other than peace or joy, we've been attacked in our mind by the evil one. It begins with a seed thought in our mind.

Warren Wiersbe asks, "Why would Satan want to attack your mind? Because your mind is the part of the image of God where God communicates with you and reveals His will to you. It is unfortunate that some Christians have minimized the significance of the mind, because the Bible emphasizes its importance. If Satan can get you to believe a lie, then he can begin to work in your life to lead you into sin. This is why we must protect our minds from the attacks of the wicked one."

How do we protect our minds?

God's admonition is: "Watch over your heart"—in Jewish thinking "the heart" was the same as the mind—"with all diligence, for from it flows springs of life" (Proverbs 4:23). The best way to protect our minds is to have the mind of Christ (I Corinthians 2:16). How do we have the mind of Christ? By renewing it daily in the Word of God (Romans 12:2). Exchanging lies for truth. We can be more than conquerors because of who Christ is in our lives (Romans 8:37).

Secondly, Christians have positional authority over Satan. Our position and power is Jesus Christ. For victory we must speak God's Word out loud to Satan. He is not able to read our minds. A great example in Scripture is when our Lord Jesus Christ was tempted by Satan in the wilderness (Matthew 4:1–10). Jesus spoke the Scripture out loud to Satan. He met every temptation with Scripture because He was God. You and I have the same choice because *of* God and our authority *through* Christ (Ephesians 1:18–21).

If you do not know the Scriptures well, you can still appropriate your authority *in* Christ. For instance, "Satan, leave me alone. I command you by the power of Jesus Christ and His shed blood on the cross to flee from me. I have decided to trust God in all things." I can assure you, Satan will flee at the very mention of His name. But he isn't able to read our minds. That is why we must rebuke him verbally.

Spiritual erosion

As we go back to the story of the prodigal son in Luke 15, I don't think the son's decision to make a life change took place overnight. Spiritual erosion takes time. But it begins in the mind. He probably had thoughts of jealousy, envy, and pride. He may have started hearing about a life he'd never experienced, so his life at home started looking dull. Boredom is a dangerous thing! He might have thought about how great it would be to kick up his heels. Meet new people. Try something new. Yet the more one thinks about wandering away from God, the more the enemy paints it as beautiful and fun.

Remember how the enemy manipulated King David's thoughts and actions? David was a very ordinary boy when he was a shepherd growing up on the farm. Then David became a somebody. He became a giant-killer. He became wealthy. He became a king. He was a warrior. Yet David was still just an ordinary man who had an extraordinary relationship with God. The Scripture says he was a man after God's own heart! But spiritual erosion set in, and he got bored. A bored mind is a dangerous thing. Satan loves it! David became proud. He had everything. The kingdom was united and Saul was defeated! David let down his guard. The enemy painted something beautiful, all right; her name was Bathsheba. One night David watched her bathing from his rooftop and, well … you know the rest of the story. He could have turned around and run inside. But he'd been *had*. So he chose to satisfy his flesh and walked away from God. From that point on everything changed.

David became a womanizer and someone who arranged the death of Bathsheba's husband so he could marry her. David was just an ordinary man who went down fast, just like the rest of us can. Anyone can walk away from God.

For an entire year, David, the mighty king of Israel, did not repent. He covered his sin. But then, David finally spoke the truth: "I have sinned against the Lord" (Psalms 51:4). He made no excuses. He did not blame anyone else! He didn't blame his parents. He didn't blame Bathsheba. He didn't blame her choice for where she took a bath! He took all the responsibility on himself and said, "The problem is me!" *That's* genuine repentance.

Spiritual erosion and the world system

Would you agree that our country is in a state of spiritual erosion? That some people are a bit bored? Satan has sabotaged it and occupied the territory. It hasn't happened over night, but there has been a steady decline. It's hard to believe what's happened in the last ten years. The list is too long to complete, but permit me to name a few things:

* God's plan for the family is falling apart. The divorce rate in the church is the same as that outside the church.
* There seems to be an agenda to expose our children to sex earlier and earlier. The media are drenched in sexual innuendoes, blatant at times.
* Much of the lyrics in today's secular music are sexual and filthy. Rap music is merely pornographic poetry that is XX-rated. Adolescents can download the very lyrics mom and dad forbid.
* Pornography is available at the touch of a computer key.

* There are X-rated movies and videos on cable. TV sitcoms not only encourage sexual immorality, they make a joke of it. Some animated movies are PG-13 because of sexual content!

* The dominating themes of many of the movies center on evil and the supernatural. They are also saturated in darkness.

* Many children have been exposed to evil and demons through sources of witchcraft and cultic teachings.

* Hard rock music and concerts are exposing people to demonic invasion, music filled with themes of suicide.

* Musicians encourage children and young adults to rebel against parental authority. Today, black is white and up is down.

* Peer pressure is a huge predicament.

* Today living together outside the bonds of marriage is accepted and encouraged as normal. Lavish weddings are in, staying married is out!

* The sanctity of marriage between a man and a woman is being questioned.

* Occultic and demonic video games abound.

* Board games that attract demons, such as Dungeons and Dragons, and Ouija boards are popular.

* Comic books and posters that have these same themes are dangerous for young people, as they draw them little by little into deeper levels of the glorification of violence.

* Teens and young adults emulate rock musicians, movie stars, celebrities, and athletes who lead lives of self-absorption, decadence, and greed.

✻ Using illegal drugs has become a way of life in America. Many lobby for legalization of certain drugs.

Add to all of this the saddening truth that America is trying to take God out of everything!

Timothy said that in the last days difficult times would come. No parent would argue that these are difficult times. "For men will be lovers of self, lovers of money, boastful, arrogant, revilers, disobedient to parents, ungrateful, unholy, unloving, irreconcilable, malicious gossips, without self-control, brutal haters of good, treacherous, reckless, conceited lovers of pleasure rather than lovers of God" (2 Timothy 3:1–5 NASB).

Be enlightened, but do not be discouraged. God is still in control, and is still more powerful than anything or anyone, including Satan.

Steps to getting on with your life ... *and* winning the war!

✻ We are not unloving if we separate ourselves from our prodigal! Separating protects love, because we are taking a stand against the things that destroy love.

✻ Remember, God does not reward His children when they are living in sin, but He never stops loving us.

✻ You are in a spiritual war, but don't be afraid; it's winnable through Christ.

✻ The battle begins in the mind. If you are experiencing fear, discouragement, despair, and defeat ... you are being attacked.

* How are you set free? Change the way you think. If you don't take captive your thoughts back to Christ, the enemy will take you captive with your own thoughts … and emotions.
* Exercise the authority Christ gave you over the evil one (Luke 10:17).
* Your prodigal is being influenced by Satan, the culture, spiritual erosion, and the flesh. These are powerful forces, but *not* more powerful than God.
* Make a decision: "I choose to be strong in the Lord and the strength of His might" (Ephesians 6:10).
* Submit yourself then to God. "Resist the devil, and he will flee from you. Come near to God and he will come near to you" (James 4:7–8a).

The spiritual weapons against the forces of darkness I wrote about in this chapter are God's Word and prayer. The full armor of God (Ephesians 6)! In Chapters 7 and 8, we will address in depth how to appropriate these weapons so you can get on with life and live in victory.

"If I take Jesus as my Lord, I take the devil on as my enemy."

—Michael Green

Chapter Five

The Power of the Pigpen

"If I had to choose between pain and nothing,
I would choose pain."
—William Faulkner

YEARS AGO I met a gal with a brother who had been a drug addict *and* a drug dealer. The family bailed him out of one pigpen after another for more than twelve years. He went from one rehab program to another, on Dad's dime, but never stayed sober very long. Like most parents, they were consumed with their addicted son, and literally put their lives on hold for years and years trying to help him change. He was draining their bank account. No matter what they did, his life was constant chaos. They had three other thriving, healthy, successful children whom they almost ignored.

Then the dad suffered a fatal heart attack, and Mom was left alone to deal with her prodigal. Or so she thought!

Soon after the funeral this prodigal son called his mom for help again. But this time my friend Becky answered the phone.

"Hi, is Mom there?"

"Yes, but you cannot speak to her. Your sister, brother, and I have made a decision to protect Mom from your manipulation and deception. You are draining her emotionally and financially. Someone has to protect her, and I have chosen to be that person."

"Whadayamean?" he screamed at the top of his lungs, followed by a stream of expletives. "I need some blankety-blank help here. I just read about an unbelievable rehab program and if you can just get me into it I know I can get clean and sober for good. Please, please, I need you to do that for me."

"Matt, if you want to get clean and sober, crawl to it on your belly in the gutter if you have to, but get help *yourself*. We are finished bailing you out! You are not a little boy anymore. No one else can make you want sobriety. We've tried over and over again to help restore your life. If you want to be sober, get sober. Until you do, stop ruining our mother's life. Stop calling her!"

Tough words? Absolutely! Filled with lots of unconditional love and tenderness? Yes and no! But sisters have a lot less to lose emotionally when it comes to siblings. She and her sister and brother were stepping in to protect their vulnerable mom from Matt's continually taking advantage of her.

The good news is that it worked. The power of the pigpen worked! Matt ran out of enablers and options and had to experience consequences. Matt had run out of painkillers! He had to be kicked out of his comfort zone in order to get his attention. It seems he had to beg the head of the rehab program to let him in, but he wouldn't give up! He was serious about change. He was sick of his life. Through the program he gave his life to Christ and was delivered from drinking and drugs. He's been sober for thirty years. It was tough love and the pigpen that changed his mind, and Jesus Christ who changed his life.

Tough love and tough stuff

Sadly, the principle of sowing and reaping is not allowed in many prodigals' lives. Parents naturally want to help, but it turns into enabling or rescuing, and nothing changes. There are no consequences. So why should prodigals change? They can have life both ways. One foot in the pigpen and the other in their parents' pockets, and their home. Ask yourself, "Has what I've been doing in the past worked? Has enabling and taking care of everything to ensure our prodigal's comfort stood in the way of repentance?"

Phil Waldrep says this to parents of prodigals: "Attempting to fix all our children's problems can be more devastating for them than we realize. It may bring temporary relief, but in the long run it prevents them from learning valuable lessons that can change their lives."

A far-off land

When the prodigal starts out on his journey to a far-off land, he's running right into Satan's territory. I think we can paint a far-off land any way we want to.

Jesus doesn't tell us any of the minute details of what the boy in the parable did. But we can well imagine some of the things that happen. However, there does come a day when he's finished living it up; he reaches into his pocket and finds there isn't a thing left. He is flat broke.

Now he's in a horrible mess financially, and the country is in a famine. The places where he thought the grass was greener have dried up. He doesn't know what to do. He may have sought the help of all the friends he had when times were good, but now he finds them to be fair-weather friends. You know the kind.

"I'd like to help you but I'm having it tough, too. And besides, why didn't you set aside some money for a rainy day? Hey, it's not my fault you are in the mess you are in today!"

This boy goes from place to place looking for help, but times are grave.

The prodigal's sin costs him so much he is *starving*. Can't find anything to eat. Maybe he thinks about sending word home to his dad asking for more cash. But the father would refuse, because he loves his son too much to underwrite him in his rebellion and sin. So, he finds a citizen of the land and asks him for help, but he can't promise him any pay because of the famine. So he gets a job raking out a pigpen (Luke 15:15–16).

I have to stop and ask you a question: Have you ever smelled pig poop?

In the early years of our marriage, we lived in a duplex close to the college campus. Our next-door neighbors lived in a tiny, run-down home. They could be classified as eccentric, to say the least. We didn't really know them, but waved occasionally.

One Saturday morning we were awakened by a gagging odor invading our nostrils and changing the color of our faces to green.

"Oh my gosh, what on earth is that?" my husband said as he grimaced.

"Oh, pew! That's worse than a cat box. Where on earth is that coming from?" I asked, gagging.

We tiptoed around our house, thinking the sewer had backed up into our tub or some ugly creature had died in one of the rooms, or our attic. The ghastly odor increased as we got closer to the front door. We opened the door and were nearly knocked off our precious little feet.

"Our neighbor has spread something all over his lawn," my husband said, as he covered his mouth and nose with his hand.

"Let me see, let me see!" I said as I squeezed next to him.

"I think it's something he took from an outhouse!"

My husband decided to get dressed and go have a talk with him.

"Hey, how ya doing?" he asked, not really wanting to know.

"Great! Just getting the yard greened up for the summer!"

"Really, what are you using?"

"Pig manure," he bragged.

"*Pig manure?* I've never heard of anyone using pig manure on a lawn. Why?"

"Cuz someone done gave it to me free! Want some?"

That's like asking someone if they'd like to tour a sardine factory two weeks after the refrigeration shut down.

My husband shook his head, declined the offer, and walked back to our house as quickly as he could.

"Hey, my friend has plenty if you change yer mind."

My husband never changed his mind. But he wanted as far away from that stench as possible. Even though the weather was quite mild outside, he turned the air conditioner on full blast.

The stench from pig manure or a pigsty is powerful. Most folks will do anything to get away from it.

The stench of sin

Prodigals living in the pigpen have turned their backs on God. This kind of living has a stench of its own. The emptiness of a heart and life apart from God is not a sweet aroma. This state is very effective and powerful if parents don't step in and rake up the muck. It is in this place that people start coming to their senses.

In the story of the prodigal, please know that for this young man to want to eat *anything* those pigs put in their mouth *confirms* his starving state. But the problem was, the kind of food pigs can digest is impossible for humans to digest. You've heard the expression "not fit for human consumption"? The food used to feed these swine was carob pods. The human digestive system can't handle it. So even if he could have beaten the pigs to their food, his stomach would have rejected it.

When this story was told by Jesus, every Israelite, both Pharisee and publican, who was listening to Him must have winced because a Hebrew couldn't go any lower than that. He was to have *nothing* to do with swine (Mosaic law had shut him off from them), but to stoop to the place where he'd go down and live with them was horrifying! That's the picture, and it's a black picture. You see this boy had hit the very bottom.

The prodigal's situation couldn't have been more grave. Yet the father stayed put! He did *not* run after his son and fill his pockets with money, or his tummy with food.

A changed mind

Why does the prodigal go home? Does he realize the servants have it better than he does? Does he realize he needs to get home? Is it because he has shamed his father and wants to make it right? Is it because he misses his older brother? Is it because pangs of guilt lurk under the surface? Is it his heart that drives him home? What drives him to his senses? It is his *stomach!* The prodigal goes home because he is hungry (Luke 15:17). His hunger changes his thinking. It makes him realize the life he once enjoyed is over. He sees that his father's servants have it better off than he does. Hunger drives him home. Home to his father. Home to confess his sins, his sins against his father and against God. Hunger makes him feel disgust about himself. He doesn't think he is fit to still be called a son. He asks his dad to let him be one of the hired hands (Luke 15:18–19).

Steps to getting on with your life

* ❊ Let the power of the pigpen do its work in your prodigal's life! Pain is a great teacher.

* ❊ Parent, let the principle of sowing and reaping take place in your prodigal's life.

* ❊ The father in the parable of the prodigal son did *not* underwrite his son's rebellion or his sin. He loved him too much.

* ❊ Pain and hunger changed the prodigal's thinking. It brought him to his senses. Parent, the goal of tough love is a restored life.

* ❊ "Those who have been bailed out time and time again develop calluses over their hearts. Each time it adds another layer and makes it even more diffi-cult for the prodigal to soften his heart. But noth-ing is too difficult for God," according to Phil Waldrep.

"Many of the right things to do in life are the most difficult to do."

—Norm Wright

Chapter Six

Where Do You Run for Answers?

"Men give advice; God gives wisdom."
—Leonard Ravenhill

YEARS AGO WE met a couple who had a very rebellious son. They shared their story with us.

"We tried everything we could think of to stop the downward spiral. As time went by, Carl fell deeper and deeper into the world of darkness. He got some tattoos, a nose ring, a tongue ring, died his hair an odd color, wore belts with spikes, and engaged in unthinkable activities. He distanced himself daily from us. He distanced himself from God, too.

"Like most parents, we were desperate for some help! We knew he was into drugs and headed for disaster. All reason, restriction, and rules had absolutely no effect on his life.

"We investigated a lot of options and finally decided we would send him to this secular drug-rehab program in another state. It was endorsed by many people as having the highest success ratio for getting kids off drugs and alcohol. The cost of the one-year, intense program was astronomical, but we were willing to jeopardize our own financial future to get our son well. We took out a second mortgage on our home.

"After much protesting from Carl, he had no choice but to go through with this rigid plan. Once he reached the rehab center he was unable to contact us for several weeks due to an 'isolation' period. It was part of the discipline and strict routine. It was the hardest time in our lives.

"After several months he was allowed visitors, and we flew down to spend time with him. He seemed better, but he was extremely bitter that we could send him away to such a place. 'You've treated me like a common criminal. Some parents you are!'

"'We are only doing this for your good, son.'

"After one year in the program, he was pronounced 'clean, sober, and rehabilitated.' Carl couldn't wait to get back home.

"Yet within a few weeks of leaving the rigid routine of the program, he drifted back to his old friends, and the comfort of the drugs. He was powerless over their strong hold on his life," they said in tears.

Much like the woman who was willing to spend $200,000 for someone to cure her son, this couple financed their future to do the same thing. This huge sacrifice led to failure, and they fell into despair.

I think the parents' motives were pure, but the program was lacking something. It was simply teaching their son behavior modification. But the flesh cannot be managed. Prodigals need supernatural power from within to find freedom. This power comes from Jesus Christ, in a heart that is hungry for change.

The original twelve-step program was begun in the early twentieth century. It was based on the twelve steps of sanctification. Sadly, many programs today leave Jesus Christ out and have added humanism and self-help. There is no power in our fallen flesh. Real freedom is found through Christ alone.

Dead Ends

When we first started out with a prodigal, we began by overlooking the problem. Denial! Pain avoidance! It's a common response. Then we tried to help. It turned into endless help. Then we looked outside our own understanding for some answers. We ran into a lot of dead ends.

We started reading self-help books, hoping for some answers. But we learned that our self (the flesh) is weak and our hearts are wicked. Self can't help. Self is what got our world into the mess it's in today. We gave up on that.

We read many books on how to get along with a prodigal, how to parent a prodigal, and how to live with a prodigal. But they offered no permanent relief. Things only grew worse.

Then we checked out secular psychology. We made an appointment and went for help. But the counsel (we later learned) did not line up with God's Word. It was actually counsel based on godless assumptions and evolutionary foundations, which are really only capable of dealing with people superficially and on a temporal level. The self-indulgent pursuit of things like self-esteem and self-fulfillment are shallow and fleeting. The counselor called sin a sickness. This counsel left us confused more than comforted.

God said to Job, "Who is this that darkens counsel by words without knowledge?"(Job 42:3). What are words without knowledge? They are words that do not line up with the Scripture.

Do you know what the word "psychology" means? True psychology is the study of the soul. It is not a bad thing. But Christians are the only ones equipped to do *soul* work, because Christians are the only ones who have the resources! The resources are the power of the Holy Spirit and God's Word, and an understanding of the transforming power of the soul.

In I Corinthians 2:14 we read that the *natural* man does not accept the things of the Spirit of God, for they are foolishness to him, and he cannot understand them, because they are spiritually appraised. So ... we know that the Scripture is written to the *Christian,* and only a believer can understand it! It's the *manual* for "soul work" and is so comprehensive in the diagnosis and treatment of every spiritual matter that, energized by the Holy Spirit in the believer, it leads to freedom and biblical sanctification.

It is good to remember that all of our soul problems are because of our sinful flesh (Romans 7:17–18).

A trained counselor has certain techniques that help people communicate better, and understand human behavior, but the key that unlocks the door and leads one to spiritual freedom is taking the hand of God, and learning Truth.

"There is a misconception that some problems are psychological and some are spiritual," notes Neil Anderson. "As though there is a division between the human soul and spirit. But that does not exist. There is no inner conflict which is not psychological, because there is never a time when your mind, emotions, and will are not involved. Similarly, there is no problem that is not spiritual. There is no time when God is not present or when it is safe for you and me to take off the armor of God."

Heavenly counselor

Now I would be misread if I came across categorically castigating all counseling or rehabilitation.

I would also be misunderstood if I came across denying that *some* people have chemical imbalances and medical disorders.

My biggest concern is that God is often the last resort a parent runs to with problems, even though He has *all* the answers. He is the Great Physician, Wonderful Counselor, and our Heavenly Comforter. God is not a therapist. He is not just someone you approach to make it through a difficult time. He is Lord and Savior.

Counsel (or soul work) energized by the Holy Sprit and grounded in the Scripture is something we *all* need our entire lives. The wise man *should* seek and heed godly counsel. But the counsel should come from people who *know* His precepts, His attributes, the doctrines of the Christian faith, His character, His sufficiency, and our position in Christ. We cannot get enough of it! Since all of our problems are spiritual, seeking counsel from biblical counseling ministries within the Body of Christ is the wisest thing a believer can do. Go to people gifted to encourage someone with love, discernment, comfort, and the desire to restore.

"A wise man will hear and increase in learning and a man of understanding will acquire wise counsel" (Proverbs 1:5).

Steps to getting on with you life

* God has the answer for every problem we have (James 1:5).
* Behavior modification programs don't change hearts.
* Seek and then heed godly counsel in dealing with your prodigal, counsel that is anchored in Truth and encourages you to run to God. This is where victory is found.

"A season of suffering is a small price to pay for a clear view of God."

—Max Lucado

Chapter Seven

A Firm Foundation

"The sacred page is not meant to be the end, but only the means toward the end, which is knowing God Himself.

—A. W. Tozer

KAY ARTHUR, THE well-known bible teacher, tells the story of her prodigal son. She kept it a secret for years. She called it her "hidden heartache."

"Tommy was a 'beloved adversary' who tried to discredit my name, my God, and His calling upon my life.

"My husband and I cried out to God for him. Again and again I beseeched God on behalf of my firstborn. The only time in my life I ever journaled was when he was about to break my heart.

"I bent over backward trying to please this young man I loved so much. I did all I could to turn him around. But nothing worked. On top of it all I had to deal with envy as I watched other mothers whose sons loved the Lord. At other times I relived my own failures over and over until I was exhausted. Then I'd run back and cling to His promise in Romans 8:28–30: 'And we know that God causes all things to work together for good to those who love God, to those who are called according to His purpose. For whom He foreknew, He also predestined to become conformed to the image of His Son, that He might be the first-born among many brethren; and whom He predestined, these He also called; and whom He called, these He also justified; and whom He justified, these He also glorified.'

"One day the Lord just spoke to me ... not audibly, but in quietness to my heart. He said, 'Are you going to live by the things you've taught or not?' And I heard Him say, 'Be still, and know that I am God.' To be still means to cease striving, to let go, to relax.

"So I shut up and quit trying to straighten Tommy out. I just started listening and loving him unconditionally and persevering in prayer and studying His Word. As a matter of fact, I think my prayers became more fervent, because I was shut up to everything but God. What intimacy this brings ... what dependence!

"God had me right where He wanted me ... right where I needed to be."

Then the day came when Jesus set our thirty-eight-year-old son free from a lifetime of immorality and gave him a passionate love for God the Father, for God's Word, and for God's people ... and, hallelujah, for his Mama! My joy knew no bounds. I stood in awe (as others did) at the miracle of it all, for God had truly transformed our son."

Kay's story encouraged me, and convinced me. I was encouraged that she let God work. I was also very encouraged because her son came to know Christ.

I was discouraged because we spent years *not* letting God work. We found trusting God difficult. Why? It's difficult to trust someone you don't know intimately. I loved Jesus Christ, but knew little of His Word. So essentially

His Word made me miserable so I'd seek Truth to be set free.

The Bible is no ordinary book

Maybe you are asking, "Why it is so crucial to learn God's Word? How can God's Word help change my situation with my prodigal?"

Well, for starters, the Scripture is God breathed (2 Tim 3:16). Psalm 19 speaks of the power of His Word and how perfect it is. Perfect meaning whole and sufficient. It goes on to say it imparts wisdom, it's pure, and enlightens the eyes. It's true and altogether righteous. David said it was more desirable than gold. It is useful for teaching, rebuking, correcting, and training in righteousness, so that the man of God may be thoroughly equipped for every good work! The Word is living. That means it isn't some dusty old book, it's alive with His power. Every time we open it, God speaks to us personally and differently depending on our need! "The sum of Your Word is truth, and every one of Your righteous ordinances is everlasting" (Psalms 119:160). "The Word of God is living and active and sharper than any two-edged sword, and piercing as far as the division of soul and spirit, of both joints and marrow, and able to judge the thoughts and intentions of the heart" (Hebrews 4:12).

Nothing gives us *conviction* like Truth. It renews and transforms our minds. It comforts us when we are hurting. It gives us hope. It gives us a fresh, heavenly perspective! But more importantly, dear parent, it brings *freedom*.

Jesus said, "If you continue in my word, then are you my disciples indeed; and you shall know the truth, and the truth shall make you free" (John 8:32).

The Psalmist knew how the Word set him free: "If Your law had not been my delight, then I would have perished in my affliction. I will never forget Your precepts, for by them you have revived me" (Psalms 119:92–93).

Parent, would you like a fresh start, a revival of your life and heart that has been on hold for so long? The way you *think* determines the way you *feel*, and the way you feel influences the way you act.

The whole counsel of God

The only way we can get a fresh start and receive transforming power to get through the storms of life is to get into the Scripture for ourselves, to study it in its *entire* context! I cannot overemphasize this crucial decision. God's Word will provide the pathway to living a victorious life, instead of looking for it through your children, or circumstances.

As you begin to learn God's Word and recognize your position in Christ Jesus, then you will never fail in your power over the enemy. You are seated in heavenly places above all the powers of the enemy (Ephesians 1:18–23). He will try to lure you away from your position of faith any time he can get you to act independently of Christ. But you are going to become a valiant warrior against the forces of darkness!

This is great news, isn't it? To think that God has allowed all your pain so you have an appetite for His Word, and exercise its authority against demonic forces that have trapped you in a prison of emotions! You'll find that you want to know Him better and more intimately than ever before. Once you have this hunger to learn truth, it means you have been humbled ... then His power is unleashed.

Basic training

As with any new regimen, we have to go through basic training. Someone who decides to run a marathon doesn't lace up his shoes and start running twenty-six miles the first day. He begins slowly, methodically. He builds up his endurance by getting into a routine. Anything worthwhile takes time, endurance, perseverance, and a routine. It's also a lot of work.

God wanted to teach both my husband and me how to jump-start the maturing process in our spiritual lives. But we had to make a choice do our part.

Are you ready to make this choice? Ready to enter basic training? It's going to be a great experience. It means rolling up your sleeves and digging into His Word.

Barbara Johnson said, "When we're down in the valley, that's where we're going to grow because that is where the fertilizer is. That's where [we] have to seek out God's help."

I think of how Job went through so much pain and darkness. He was in the valley all right, yet he was able to say, "By his light I walked through darkness" (Job 29:3).

A plan to grow

I have a confession to make. It's just the way I am wired. I have to have a plan to grow. I need direction. For years people admonished me to get into the Bible for myself, but I confess, I didn't know where to begin! I'd either get bogged down in an Old Testament book, or lose my place and then give up. I tried the hunt and peck method. You know, close your eyes, open the Bible, and then point your figure on a page and wherever your finger lands, that's where to read. But I never grasped the *context* of the entire Bible.

I was so thrilled when someone recommended the one-year Bible to me. It's even called *The One-Year Bible*. The reason I clarify this is because after a gal heard me recommend it at a conference, she misunderstood me. She went to the bookstore and asked for the Bible written by Judy Hampton.

The One-Year Bible is dated, starting in January. Obviously you can begin today. Each day there are a few chapters from the Old Testament, a few chapters from the New Testament, a Psalm, and some Proverbs. It takes approximately 15 minutes a day to read through the Bible in a year. It comes in many versions. I recommend starting with the New Living Translation. Reads like a newspaper.

Now, if you should miss a day or two, don't go back. It's as though the enemy whispers, "Don't read this, it's out of date ... besides, you'll never catch up now." But you can catch up next year. Just keep going!

God used a wise person's words to convince me. "Judy, do you have fifteen minutes to read God's Word, receive His instruction, comfort, and counsel? Because if you don't, you might want to reevaluate your life."

I was convinced fifteen minutes a day was doable. However, I quickly found myself hungering for more than fifteen minutes. That's when I knew He was drawing me into His presence more and more.

Rick Warren's counsel is: "Don't worry how fast you grow, God is concerned about how *strong* we grow."

A changed perspective

As my husband and I began to learn God's Word it changed our perspective. Our perception of God had come

72

from our past and even harmful relationships. Our perception of God must come from his Word, nothing else! David understood this. He asked the Lord to guide him in all truth and teach him (Psalms 25:5).

We first began to learn about God's character. Imagine knowing Christ as savior, and *not* understanding or knowing His character. Yep, we were in training!

We learned that God knows all because He is omniscient. He knew before the world began that we'd be in the midst of this mess with our prodigal ... and He would be there for us!

He is omnipotent, which means He is all-powerful. He can do anything ... including change our children.

He is eternal, always the same. He *never* changes! What stability this brings to His children who are in the midst of uncharted waters.

He in incomprehensible and good! Now I know why He tells me to thank Him in all things! Because He is good, and all things are for a reason.

He is self-existent. He Himself is God. He is self-sufficient, able to act. He can move mountains, but He'd rather move you and me ... closer to Himself!

He is infinite and has no limits or bounds. I am grateful that no man can thwart God's hand or plan (Job 42:2).

He is transcendent, above all creation. He is holy, morally perfect, good, fair, compassionate, slow to anger, knows the beginning from the end, and gave Himself for us! These amazing character qualities give me such confidence to know that He knows everything that is going on, everywhere, and can change it anytime!

He is unconditional, and hates unrighteousness. Wow! God deals with our sin, but His love is unconditional.

He is truthful, faithful, and will not share the glory. This is a picture of our Most High God. (All Scriptures on the sovereignty of God are in the Notes at the end of this book.)

Our new perspective of God showed us why we can put all our confidence in Him.

A wise teacher once said, "If we don't understand the character of God, we will not be able to embrace the sovereignty of God when the bottom falls out of our life."

Then we began to learn the promises of God! It has been said there are some thirty-seven thousand promises in the Word of God. Imagine this. They are *ours* for the asking! And God is able to make good on all of them.

As I began to grasp the sovereignty of God, I began to rest in it. I no longer had confidence in myself, but was filled with hope that God had allowed everything, including a prodigal, to do a work in me.

"Man shall not live by bread alone, but on every word that proceeds out of the mouth of God"(Matthew 4:4).

Unity in pain

The Scriptures brought my husband and me closer than we'd ever imagined. Unity! This is such praise! We became so connected as we shared this trial. We were encouraging one another, praying for one another, and supporting one another. Oh, sure, there were some nights we held each other tightly and had a good cry. It's the reality of our humanity, and our love for our children. But may I challenge you *not* to take sides and allow your children to come between you and your spouse? Prodigals are often consumed with self, and are not giving any thought to your marriage. Guard against this! Become a team; stop blaming each other and let God use this time to build your relationship and make it rock-solid.

When I first memorized the verse "Consider it all joy, my brethren, when you experience various trials" (James 1:2–3), I admit it sounded a bit harsh because our hearts were breaking and we were not yet joyful. But looking back now I can assure you that it's possible to "consider it all joy" because it's *not* the final curtain call in your life or your prodigal's life. It is actually a new beginning. God is producing perseverance and hope in you. It's possible to consider it all joy because if the Lord commands anything of us, He also provides what we need in order to live it out. If this trial were not for your benefit and His glory, He would never have allowed it to seep into your life through His sovereign fingers of incredible love.

"Friends, when life gets really difficult, don't jump to the conclusion that God isn't on the job. Instead, be glad that you are in the very thing of what Christ experienced. This is a spiritual refining process, with glory just around the corner" (I Peter 4:12).

Going forward with confidence

As God began changing us, slowly the fog lifted from our clouded thinking. As we were His children, He was refining us. He was kicking us out of our nursery-like faith and growing us up! His truth often makes us miserable before it really comforts us! We learned we had been predestined according to *His* purpose, He who works all things after the counsel of His will! We were *not* victims; we were in the center of His will. We could go forward and live our lives with confidence.

"For our light and momentary troubles are achieving for us an eternal glory that far outweighs them all. So we fix our eyes not on what is seen, but on what is unseen. For what is seen is temporary, but what is unseen is eternal" (2 Corinthians 4:7–10,17).

Steps to getting on with your life

✿ Put the past behind, and build a firm foundation on the Word of God. Your perception of God must come from the Scripture, not your relationship with others.

✿ Experience God's glory as you study His Word. "For in Him we live and move and have our being (Acts 17:28).

✿ If you are married, let the Word and this trial bring you closer together.

✿ Suffering makes us more and more dependent on God. His Word means more when we have run out of answers.

✿ This is where faith comes into full view. It's gut-level. It's the substance of things hoped for, the evidence of things not seen.

✿ Go forward in confidence.

"He sent His Word and healed them and delivered them from their destruction."

Psalms 107:20

Chapter Eight

Power-Packed Prayers

*Prayer is our weapon for bringing down strongholds
raised up against the knowledge of God.*

—2 Corinthians 10:3–5

JIM CYMBALA, AUTHOR and pastor, wrote of a severe test when he and his wife, Carol, went through the darkest two-and-a-half-year tunnel they could imagine.

"Our oldest daughter, Chrissy had been a model child growing up. But around sixteen she began to stray. I admit I was too slow to notice this ... I was too occupied with the church, starting branch congregations, overseeing projects, and all the rest that ministry entails.

"Meanwhile, Chrissy not only drew away from us, but also away from God. In time, she even left our home. There were many nights when we had no idea where she was.

"As the situation grew more serious, I tried everything. I begged, I pleaded, I scolded, I argued, I tried to control her with money. Looking back, I recognize the foolishness of my actions. Nothing worked; she just hardened more and more.

"Were we calling on the Lord through all of this? In a sense we were. But I couldn't help jumping in to take action on my own, too. I was still, to some degree, the point guard waiting to grab the basketball, push it down the floor, make something happen, press through any hole in the defense I could find. But the more I pressed, the worse Chrissy got.

"Once again, back in 1972, there came a divine show-down. God strongly impressed me to stop crying, scream-ing, or talking to anyone else about Chrissy. I was to con-verse with no one but God. In fact, I knew I should have no further contact with Chrissy ... until God acted. I was just to believe and obey what I had preached so often ... 'Call upon me in your time of trouble, and I will answer you.'

"I began to pray with an intensity and growing faith as never before. Whatever bad news I would receive about Chrissy, I kept from interceding and actually began praising God for what I knew he would do soon. I made no attempts to see her. Carol and I endured the Christmas sea-son with real sadness.

"February came. One cold Tuesday night during the prayer meeting, I talked from Acts 4 about the church boldly calling on God in the face of persecution. We entered into a time of prayer, everyone reaching out to the Lord simultaneously. A young woman whom I felt to be spiritually sensitive had written: 'Pastor Cymbala, I feel impressed that we should stop the meeting and all pray for your daughter.'

"I hesitated. Was it right to stop the flow of the service and focus on my personal need? Yet something in the note seemed to ring true. In a few minutes I picked up a microphone and told the congregation what had just happened. 'The truth of the matter, although I haven't talked much about it, is that my daughter is very far from God these days. She thinks up is down and down is up; dark is light, and light is dark. But I know God can break through to her, and so I'm going to ask Pastor Boekstaaf to lead us in praying for Chrissy.' To describe what happened in the next minutes, I can only employ a metaphor: *The church became a labor room.*

"Thirty-two hours later, on Thursday morning, as I was shaving, Carol suddenly burst through the door, her eyes wide. 'Go downstairs!' she blurted. 'Chrissy's here.'

"'Chrissy, here?'

"'Yes, Go down!'

"I wiped off the shaving foam and headed down the stairs, my heart pounding. As I came around the corner, I saw my daughter on the kitchen floor, rocking on her hands and knees, sobbing. Cautiously I spoke her name.

"'Chrissy?'

"She grabbed my pant leg and began pouring out her anguish. 'Daddy ... Daddy ... I've sinned against God. I've sinned against myself. I've sinned against you and Mommy. Please forgive me ...'

"My vision was as clouded by tears as hers. I pulled her up from the floor and held her close as we cried together.

"Suddenly she drew back. 'Daddy, who was praying for me? Who was praying for me?

"'In the middle of the night, God woke me and showed me I was heading toward this abyss. There was no bottom to it ... it scared me to death. I was so frightened. I realized how hard I've been, how wrong, how rebellious. But at the same time, it was like God wrapped his arms around me and held me tight. He kept me from sliding any farther as he said, 'I still love you.'

"Chrissy's life changed dramatically. Eventually she went to Bible college and began serving the Lord in music ministry. Today she is a pastor's wife in the Midwest with three wonderful children.

"Through all of this, Carol and I learned as never before that persistent calling upon the Lord breaks through every stronghold of the devil, for nothing is impossible with God. For Christians in these troubled times, there is simply no other way."

Jim Cymbala called upon God in his day of trouble. His family was in a war. But through prayer and God's Word, the battle was won.

Warfare praying

Seems like I am obsessed with spiritual warfare. But it's so vitally important to realize it isn't something to ignore or be afraid of, but a reality of the Christian life. We must *learn* to appropriate God's power through prayer.

"When we enter into a spiritual battle with the enemy, we enter into a different realm of prayer, says Kay Arthur. "This type of prayer requires standing fast ... holding our ground and not budging ... until the victory is won. To see a lack of prayer as subtle pride throws a new light on unceasing prayer, doesn't it? Remember, our battle is not against flesh and blood. It's against the powers, the world forces of this darkness, against the spiritual forces of wickedness in the heavenly places (Ephesians 6:12). Unrestrained because of the lack of fervent prayers of saints trained in warfare praying, Satan is like a high-spirited horse. You must let him know who is boss; you must keep a tight rein. You must hold the bit tightly by wrapping the reins of God's Truth firmly around your hands ... and then hold and not let go until Satan and his demons come to total submission to the truths of God's Word."

This *is* the key to victory! Hold the reins of God's Truth firmly until Satan and his demons come to total submission to God's Word!

"Let us then approach the throne of grace with confidence, so that we may receive mercy and find grace to help us in our time of need" (Hebrews 4:16). The inheritance of every Christian is "authority ... over all the powers of the enemy" (Luke 10:17–20).

God used a dear friend of mine to call my attention to this very neglected area of my life. She lovingly pointed out the importance of developing a powerful prayer life. She told me Jesus provided a way for us to enter the Holy of Holies so we could have intimate fellowship with God. Prayer isn't some duty; it's a privilege. Prayer keeps us in constant communion with God, which is the goal of our entire life! A prayerless life is a powerless life.

Remember those spiritual weapons? His Word *and* prayer! According to Beth Moore, "They are like two sticks of dynamite taped together!"

Being girded in truth

Again, I needed a plan to develop a prayer life. Not out of a sense of duty, but for obedience and power. When I don't go to the Lord in prayer, I am actually saying, "Lord, I don't want to bother you. I really believe I can handle my own problems."

Jesus said in John 15:7, "If you abide in Me, and My words abide in you, ask whatever you wish, and it will be done for you." The word "abide" means to stay close, to be with someone every day. Some refer to it as spiritual breathing.

The first step to developing a powerful prayer life is staying close to Jesus.

A plan to pray

What Jesus is saying in John 15 is simply this: If we want our prayers to make a powerful difference in our life and in the lives of our prodigals, we must pray according to the Word of God. This is praying according to the *will* of God.

If I "ask anything according to His will, and I know He hears me ... then I have the petitions desired of Him" (I John 5:14–15). God will give us a solution to our problems ... in His time.

Regardless of the type of prayer, we can have the confidence that God hears our prayers. "Call to Me and I will answer you, and show you great and mighty things which you do not know" (Jeremiah 33:3). God wants us to pray.

One great place to start praying God's Word is the Psalms. Then listen for His answer. The Psalms were written by men inspired by the Lord of the universe, full of emotional heartache, turmoil, doubt, anxiety, and fear. Let God speak to you through those Psalms. He will minister to your soul, and as you read, pray His promises back to Him.

For instance, the Psalmist knew that God would show him His will: "I will instruct you and teach you in the way you should go; I will guide you with My eye" (Psalms 32:8).

"The entrance of Your words gives light; it gives understanding to the simple" (Psalms 119:130).

"Your Word is a lamp to my feet, a light to my path" (Psalms 119:105).

The Psalmist even gave us a good time to pray. "In the morning, O Lord, you hear my voice; in the morning I lay my requests before you and wait in expectation" (Psalms 5:3).

Another great tool for praying God's Word is buying a little book of God's promises. They are available in paperback, at any Christian bookstore. The book lists His promises by category, such as promises for praising Him, for suffering, for the family, for discouragement, for wisdom, and for thanksgiving.

I began my prayer life with praise and adoration. Praising God for who He is, not what He can do for me. Praising Him because He is the only one worthy of praise. Praising Him because He is my God. Praising Him because He is going to work this mess together for good! Our goal is to make such requests to God so that the answer gives God the glory.

I began to praise Him for His character. I began to make the Scripture personal as I prayed, such as I Chronicles 29:11–12:

"Lord, I praise You today that everything in the heavens and the earth is Yours O Lord, and this is your kingdom. I take confidence in knowing that, Lord, You created me, You created my prodigal, and You can change us both! I adore you as being in control of *everything*. I thank you that I am not a victim. Thank you for allowing this trial, and time of heartache, testing, and pain. Use it to change me, Lord. Riches and honor come from you alone, and you are the ruler of all mankind; your hand controls power and might, and it is at your discretion that men are made great

83

and given strength. Oh, Father, it is You who changes man, and it is You who gives us strength. Thank You, God. You are all-powerful and able to do all things!"

"Lord, your Word says to call upon You when I am troubled, and You will answer. Lord, this family is in trouble." (Psalm 50:15).

"Oh Lord, You say in your Word that you are close to those whose hearts are breaking. Lord be near to me, minister to my breaking heart" (Psalm 34).

A clean heart

* ❖ "For a successful season of prayer, the best beginning is confession," says Charles Haddon Spurgeon.
* ❖ Confessing our sin restores *fellowship* with God.
* ❖ Jealously, a critical spirit, gossip, anger, unforgiveness, grudges, revenge, pride, self-pity, and fear are but a few sins we must address. "If we claim we have no sin, we deceive ourselves and the truth is not in us. If we confess our sins, He is faithful and just and will forgive us our sins and purify us from all unrighteousness" (I John 1:8–9).
* ❖ Idol worship is something we as parents struggle with, too. Trying to find life in another person is idol worship.
* ❖ God resists the proud (James 4:6). He draws near to the humble. We must come to God with a humble, teachable heart.
* ❖ Unbelief destabilizes us. "But when he asks, he must believe and not doubt, because he who doubts is like a wave of the sea, blown and tossed by the wind. That man should not think he will receive anything from the Lord; he is double-

minded man, unstable in all he does" (James 1:6a).

* A lack of harmony with our spouse hinders a prayer life (I Peter 3:7).
* Refusing to forgive is also a sin (Mark 11:25–26).
* Immorality shuts down the flow of the Holy Spirit ... and breaks fellowship with God, thus hindering a prayer life. God would never go against His holy, moral character and honor the prayers of one who is living in immorality.
* I am learning to ask God to reveal any sins I need to confess.

Making requests known to god

I began to paraphrase Scripture to make it personal. "Lord, your Word tells us that if any of us lacks wisdom, let him ask of You who gives to all liberally and without reproach, and it will be given to him. Lord, give us wisdom in dealing with our prodigal. Teach us what to do, how to respond, when to stay away, when to help" (James 1:5).

"Father, You ask me to submit to You, to resist the devil and he will flee. Upon Your authority given to me, I resist Satan, and command him to get out of my mind and life" (James 4:7).

"Lord, my soul wants to wait patiently for You to act, for my expectation can only be from You. Give me patience, for your timing for restoration is perfect" (Psalms 62:5).

"Father, I know with confidence that You began a good work in me, and I ask that You will be faithful to complete it. I pray you will complete the work you began in my prodigal as well" (Phil. 1:6).

"Father, your Word says that out of your kindness it leads me to repentance. Oh God, out of your kindness, please lead my prodigal to genuine repentance and new life" (Romans 2:4b).

"Father, You say you know how to deliver the godly out of temptations and to reserve the unjust under punishment for the Day of Judgment. Father, I pray you will deliver my prodigal out of temptation. Deliver me from the temptation to doubt You" (2 Peter 2:9).

"Father, we are passing through rough waters, and You say you will be with us and they will not sweep over us. When we walk through the fire, we will not be burned, and the flames will not set us ablaze. Oh Father, what an amazing, powerful God you are during this time of testing in your refining fire. May we come through as pure gold. Father, do your refining work in our prodigal's life" (Isaiah 43:2 and Psalms 66:10 personally paraphrased).

In addition to praying God's Word, Oswald Chambers suggests, "Pray about everything; this solves the mystery of what to pray for!"

"Lord, Your Word tells me to rejoice always, pray without ceasing, in everything give thanks, for this is your will in Christ Jesus" (I Thess. 5:16–18).

We can pray all day long. Pray when we drive, when we are waiting at a red light, waiting for an appointment. When we begin to worry … we can stop the cycle by confessing it as the sin of unbelief, and start praying and taking every thought captive back to the obedience of Christ (2 Corinthians 10:5). As we pray God's Word and we see answers, we *know* God is working. His will is being done. He is faithful. Then we can begin to walk in newness of life, placing our confidence in God, not our emotions.

As I go back again to the story of the prodigal son in Luke 15, I am amazed at verse 20. The prodigal comes to his senses and decides to go back home. While the son is walking toward his home, he is a long way off, yet the father sees him coming. How does he see him coming if he is far away? I think he may have been sitting at the window or on the front porch for a long time. As he waited, I believe he was trusting God and praying for his son. This was the best thing he could do.

May I suggest you solicit your friends to join you in praying? There is power in people gathered together to pray. You might consider joining a Christ-centered support group for parents of prodigals. Or starting one! You will receive great encouragement knowing you are not alone, and others are praying with you.

Steps to getting on with you life

* Make plans to start a powerful prayer life.
* Learn to pray His Word.
* Buy a book of God's promises and pray them back to Him. "The prayers of a righteous man are powerful and effective" (James 5:16b).
* Ask trusted friends to join you in prayer. Jesus said, "For where two or three are gathered in my name, I am there in their midst" (Matthew 18:20).
* May I encourage you not to hibernate! Find a support group to bear this burden with you. "I will come down and speak with you there, and I will take of the Spirit that is on you and put the Spirit on them. They will help you carry the burden ... so that you will not have to carry it alone" (Numbers 11:17).

"By intercessory prayer we can hold off Satan from other lives and give the Holy Spirit a chance with them. No wonder Jesus put such tremendous emphasis on prayer!"

—Oswald Chambers

Chapter Nine

Complete Forgiveness

"When you forgive, you in no way change the past,
but you sure do change the future."

—Anonymous

RECENTLY I HAD the privilege of interviewing an eighty-year-old man who has been at odds with his son for many years. His son has been married several times and has made many poor choices in his life. Yet he still blames his dad for most of them.

Don confessed to me that he's tried to change his son with sermonettes, had lent him books, offered unasked-for advice, and said things out of anger. "I've really been proud, stiff-necked, and unloving at times," he said. "We've had some pretty heated, verbal battles. But no one has come out a winner! Both of us are very strong willed."

Eight years ago Don and his wife moved to a small mountain community where people vacationed or retired. His son and his wife bought a cabin close by. It seemed so ideal at the time. But then things turned sour. One night they had sharp words, a difference of opinions, and his son started blaming his dad again. All communication was eventually severed. Don was devastated not to have his son around, but all he could do was pray. During the estrangement, Don's wife died suddenly. Her death and funeral brought about temporary restoration with his son, but it was phony at best.

A few weeks after the funeral, Don's son and daughter-in-law were up at their cabin and invited him over for dinner. The evening went fairly well until Don's son started drinking. Soon he brought up the past and started blaming his dad *again* for his messed-up life.

"You never loved me! If you had been a better father, I would not have made the choices I have made."

Don became defensive! His son provoked him with ugly words, and soon it turned into a verbal war. Don told his son some things he deeply regrets. He stormed out of their house, went home and tried to go to sleep. But he couldn't sleep. The Lord had him in the woodshed.

The next day Don walked over to his son's cabin. He and his wife were sitting on their porch. Don got down on his knees and begged for forgiveness! He *owned* his sin and confessed it. He told him how much he regretted his wicked words, and how much he loved him. But his apology was met with disgust and rejection. "Get out of here, and don't come back! You make me sick!"

Don went home and wept for hours. Since that time he's written notes and letters begging for forgiveness, but they have been met with several years of deafening silence. When his son comes up to his cabin, he makes no attempt to see his dad, even though his place is a mere fifty-five feet away.

Tears welled up in Don's eyes as he said, "I'd give anything to see my son again. To make things right! But I cannot make that happen, so I have chosen to trust God."

One of the most important decisions a parent of a prodigal can ever make is how we respond to a crisis. Few things are as difficult to handle emotionally and spiritually an injustice, or people who won't own up to their part of the problem. It's times like this we can be tempted to walk away from our faith. Our actions affect all the people around us.

Next, it's time to forgive

Parent, do you feel the need to make things right with your prodigal? Or does the very thought of it make you angry?

Maybe you haven't done anything wrong in your eyes. Maybe all you've done is help. Yet you've met with false accusations, disdain, blame, and rejection. Perhaps you think your prodigal should be asking *you* for forgiveness! I understand. When someone has taken your heart out and stomped on it, it's difficult to imagine you need to forgive. I can't count the number of parents I've met with horror stories. Parents who have been physically abused and subjected to cruelty, revenge, and unbelievable manipulation. But the point is, if we do not forgive our prodigal, then it will affect us in a negative way. If we don't forgive, what we are saying is, "God, my child is more important to me than a healthy relationship with You!"

Yet God tells us to forgive.

Don has finally forgiven himself, and he's forgiven his son. But the Lord had to do it *through* him.

Complete forgiveness has nothing to do with the other person's response. We have no control over what another person does. We are told to obey and choose to forgive. The rest is up to God.

Don keeps no record of wrongs. He has no plans for revenge. He does not talk about his son in a negative way to another person. He doesn't go back over the words and anger spoken that day. He's put that behind. He prays every single day for his son and his family. And guess what? His heart is filled with peace. He has laid the matter before God, trusting Him to either work it out or grant him the grace to live the rest of his life without his son.

Yet Don told me something that blessed me beyond words.

"Judy, this is the greatest time in my life!"

One would question his sanity. But Don assured me of this.

"Whatever God chooses to remove from our lives, He'll replace it with something better. I have spent years trying to win my son's love and approval. Now I spend my time living for the Lord. I love His Word, I pray every day, and I love serving Him. I am learning firsthand what the sufficiency of Jesus Christ really is."

Don has confidence God will work in his son's life. He knows it could be after he is in heaven. But He's trusting God, not his emotions or his watch.

Prison of bitterness

Don is no longer held prisoner by what someone else thinks of him. Don lives vertically, not horizontally. In other words, he's not looking at another person to fill up his life. And he is no longer wondering why his son will not forgive him. Don has forgiven him and God has given him a full, purposeful life. That's why Don has no root of bitterness.

"Bitterness seeps into the basement of our lives like run-off from a broken sewer," writes Chuck Swindoll. "Every form of ugliness begins to float to the surface of those murky waters: prejudice and profanity, suspicion and hate, cruelty and cynicism. There is no torment like the inner torment of bitterness, which is the by-product of an unforgiving spirit. It refuses to be soothed, it refuses to be healed, and it refuses to forget. There is no prison more damaging than the bars of bitterness that will not let the battle end."

Says R. T. Kendall, "Relinquishing bitterness is an open invitation for the Holy Spirit to give you His peace, His joy, and the knowledge of His will."

Revenge is one of life's sweetest temptations, a kissin' cousin to bitterness. "Vengeance sought today shifts the offense from the one who committed the sin to the one who is handling the sin with even greater sin," according to Dan Allender.

"X-ray the world of the vengeful and behold the tumor of bitterness: black, menacing, and malignant," says Max Lucado. "Carcinoma of the spirit! Its fatal fibers creep around the edge of the heart and ravage it."

What forgiveness is not

Please do not misunderstand genuine forgiveness:

* It doesn't mean that we approve of what they did.
* It doesn't mean we excuse what they did.
* It doesn't mean we justify what they did.
* It doesn't mean we pardon what they did.
* It doesn't mean we deny what they did.
* It doesn't mean we are blind to what they did.

* It doesn't mean we forget what they did.
* It doesn't mean that we refuse to take the wrong seriously.
* It doesn't mean we have to pretend it did not hurt.
* It doesn't mean we want to spend our next vacation with them.

Just do it!

I want to encourage you to ask for forgiveness from your prodigal. If you have done or said things that were wrong as a parent, admit it. You may need to ask specifically what you need to ask forgiveness for, tough as it sounds. Be prepared! If your prodigal has harbored bitterness toward you for something you did, then ask for forgiveness. This is not the time to be a rights defender; it's time to be a truth seeker. If you have been *falsely* accused, God will be your defender. It's amazing, though, how God is honored when we own our own sin and ask for forgiveness. Compassion is a *feeling* of forgiveness, but to genuinely forgive someone means *asking* for it.

Author Philip Yancy calls forgiveness "an unnatural act." Our flesh would rather rise up and defend! But without forgiveness, our wounds will simply never heal. Sure, it's easier to nurture the pain. But if we want our wounds to start healing we must forgive. Forgiveness is an act of our will.

The consequences of not forgiving

* The Holy Spirit is grieved. "And do not grieve the Holy Spirit of God, with whom you were sealed for the day of redemption" (Eph. 4:30). An unforgiving attitude grieves the Holy Spirit and resentment takes place.

❈ You are left to yourself. A refusal to forgive means
that God stands back and lets you cope with your
problems in your own strength. Not many people
want to live that kind of life ... coping on their own
without God's help (Proverbs 14:14).

❈ You force God to become your enemy. The reason
God treats you like an enemy is because, by not forgiving others, you are really saying, "God, move
over, I want to do your job!" You crown yourself
judge, jury, and executioner, and you presume to
take God's place. (See James 4:1–4.)

❈ You have no authentic fellowship with the Father. It
is a serious matter. "If we claim to have fellowship
with Him yet walk in the darkness, we lie and do
not live by the truth" (I John 1:6).

Having addressed how important it is to forgive, I think
it's important to know that *restoration* and *reconciliation* are
two entirely different matters. Restoration means making
amends with someone. If I have made amends with someone, that doesn't necessarily mean I will have a close relationship with them. An injured person can forgive an
offender without reconciliation. But in order for there to
be genuine *reconciliation*, two people must *want* it and
both must own their own sin (Matthew 18). Reconciliation
means harmony. When we sing a song, we make melody
(hopefully). To have harmony, it takes two people. A genuine relationship cannot be built on a lie or a lack of trust.

The classic and often quoted story of Joseph in the
Book of Genesis illustrates that God intends to use our pain
for His glory because He's allowed it. That's why we can
forgive!

Joseph suffered at the hands of his family and so-called friends. Joseph's ten brothers were terribly jealous of Joseph when he was growing up. He was his dad Jacob's favorite. Now, Joseph fueled the fire because of his youthful pride. So his brothers sold him into slavery to get rid of him. His father grieved and grieved, thinking Joseph was dead. Then Joseph became a convict after being falsely accused by Pharaoh's wife. She tried to tempt him to sleep with her, and he refused, so she turned on him. He was punished for doing the right thing. But in each case, Joseph responded with a positive attitude. Those who were around Joseph very long knew he followed God. He spent seventeen years in prison ... and he'd done nothing wrong. In prison Joseph interpreted dreams for the king's cupbearer and baker. And the very things Joseph told them came true. He asked them to please remember him to the king so he could get out of jail, but the cupbearer soon forgot.

Then Pharaoh had a dream. He didn't know how to interpret it. So he asked the magicians to interpret the dream, but no one could help him out. Then the cupbearer remembered Joseph and how he interpreted dreams. In the Old Testament, God often spoke to His people through dreams. So the cupbearer told the king about Joseph. Pharaoh sent for him, and he interpreted the dream. He told him that Egypt was headed for a terrible famine, and since God had made it known to Joseph, Pharaoh put Joseph in charge of Egypt! And Joseph prepared for the famine that was coming.

Back home his brothers and his parents were running out of food, so their father, Jacob, sent the ten brothers to Egypt to buy some grain so they could eat. When they arrived, Joseph recognized them, but they didn't recognize him. Why? They thought by now he was dead.

Well, at the end of this marvelous story, the time that Joseph had been separated from his brothers did not heal all their wounds. Forgiveness did! Joseph forgave his brothers, *but* they owned up to their sin as well. It's key to understand that they *repented*! Then joyful reconciliation took place.

Through all the pain Joseph experienced, the betrayal, the lies, the false accusations, and seventeen years in prison, Joseph was used by God to plan and save a nation from famine, and save the people of Israel. We see God's hand working things together for good. He planned it all. And Joseph rested in God's sovereignty: "You intended to harm me, but God intended it for good to accomplish what is now being done, the saving of many lives" (Gen. 50:20).

I know it may seem irrational to believe God is going to use all the pain you've lived through for good. You might ask, "What is good?" Could it be that the good will be how God changes *you*? Could it be that the suffering you have gone through may be used as a platform to minister to other people in the same situation? Could the good be stepping back and watching how God brings about change in your prodigal *without* your help? We can't change another person, that's for sure! Could the good be to live out the reality of the Christ life to others, that they see Him making a difference when a heart is broken? Could it be that the good that comes out of this heartache be that your faith has been deepened and your prayer life has become powerful?

"Don't grieve God. Don't break His heart. His Holy Spirit, moving and breathing in you, is the most intimate part of your life, making you fit for Himself. Don't take such a gift for granted. Make a clean break with all cutting, backbiting, profane talk. Be gentle with one another, sensitive. Forgive one another as quickly and thoroughly as God in Christ forgave you" (Ephesians 4:30–32).

Are you ready to tell God that you trust Him to settle the score in His way and in His time? God will give you a story to share about the good things that have come out of your pain if you are willing to hang in there and let it go into His capable hands. Focus on God's goodness. Please keep in mind that God is our only security. His presence can be a source of joy and sustaining power, even in the midst of great pain, when we chose to forgive.

Steps to getting on with your life
* God tells us to forgive.
* Forgiving others produces a deeper dependence on God.
* When we forgive, the flow of God's Spirit produces freedom in our lives.
* God hears the prayers of those who forgive others.
* Forgiveness heals wounds.
* Forgiveness prevents a root of bitterness from growing into our lives.
* Forgiveness does not have anything to do with the other person's response. We forgive out of obedience to God.
* We are free to forgive because we know God's in control.
* We forgive because God has forgiven us.
* Reconciliation takes place when *both* parties own their own sin, and ask for forgiveness.

There is one final element to forgiveness. I believe it's a process! For some it's a long one, and for others it comes more quickly. But we must pray for God's blessings in the life of our prodigal. Jesus said, "But I tell you: Love your enemies and pray for those who persecute you" (Matt. 5:44).

"We are never more like God than when we forgive."

—John MacArthur

Chapter Ten

God's Heavenly Timing

*"Doing the will of God leaves me no time
for disputing His plans."*
—George McDonald

I HAVE A very dear friend whose youngest child, David, began challenging his parents at an early age. Then he began breaking their hearts when he was in junior high school. There was *always* a crisis. Problems in school, and problems getting along with other kids. Then he started living in blatant rebellion.

After high school he got a young gal pregnant just before he went off to the Army. My dear friend, Karen, was there the day his girlfriend delivered the weak, ill little boy, who died soon after his birth. Karen hoped this was the end of their heartache. But it was only a beginning.

Soon David married, but the marriage didn't make it. After his divorce he blamed his failure on his parents, and even refused to speak to them for two years. Then he married again. She was a sweet gal and David's painful past seemed behind him. Yet every now and then he'd call his mom and try to play the blame game one more time.

Karen would interrupt and say, "We are not going down that road again, David. We've gone over this time and time again. We asked you to forgive us for whatever you feel we did wrong. I remember you saying you would. But it seems when you start feeling guilty over some of the decisions you've made, you call me up and start blaming me again."

Karen and Bob learned to love their son from a distance. They knew their every word was scrutinized, and eventually it would end in a confrontational phone call, blaming them for his mistakes. No matter how hard Karen and Bob tried, they never lived up to the standard David set for them.

Karen and Bob retired a few years ago and moved to another state, away from David.

David was by now a very successful plumber and his wife, Carla, was a successful insurance broker. They were making lots of money, and were involved in a thriving church. His walk with the Lord grew, but he was never very joyful about life. His focus was always on what was wrong.

Out of the blue Karen got a call that David and Carla were moving away from town in order to buy a bigger home in a new suburb. It turned out to be a huge mistake. The long commute took its toll on Carla. David's plumbing business was doing well, but Carla couldn't deal with the daily drive. By now the real estate costs had skyrocketed in the city they left, so they couldn't move back.

After a year, they decided to move a hundred miles away to her home town in a rather remote area. She wanted to be by her family and get away from the pressures of her job. It sounded like a good plan, so David agreed.

However, he just couldn't get his plumbing business going in this small town. His wife worked at a much lesser-paying job, and soon they found themselves running out of money.

David began sinking into depression. He would not seek counsel, or see a physician. His pastor and many friends tried to help, but he refused. He found it increasingly difficult to trust God with his future.

The unthinkable!

One evening Karen had company while her husband was at a finance meeting at church. The phone rang, but she just let the call go into voice mail. Then the phone rang again and again.

"Karen, I think you'd better get that call. Maybe it's important!" her friend urged.

"Okay, Okay! But it's usually a sales call. Hello," Karen said curtly into the receiver.

"Mom, this is Bill. David killed himself today."

"What? Oh, no! Oh, my God! Oh, this can't be! No, No, this can't be true. No!" Karen screamed at the top of her lungs.

She dropped the phone. She felt faint.

Her friend picked it up and got the whole story from Karen's oldest son, Bill.

She noticed Karen gasping for air. "Karen ... you have to breathe. Take a breath, sweetheart! Breathe!"

Only a parent can imagine such a nightmare. The news shattered and devastated Bob and Karen's whole world.

"I can't believe it! Why? What happened? What more could we have done? Why wouldn't he get some help?" they asked over and over again.

David left no note. One day after his wife went to work, he went down to the basement, lay down on the couch, and ended his life!

The last chapter is in heaven

As the months passed, Bob and Karen went to a grief group. They came to realize that the nightmare of David's troubled life had finally ended. David was at peace with Jesus in his new home.

They also remembered this world is not our home. The writer of Hebrews said we do not have an enduring city, but we are looking for the city that is to come (Hebrews 13:14). The Psalmist said we are *strangers* on earth (Psalms 119:19). Peter called us aliens (I Peter 2:11). Life here on earth is a temporary assignment. Our final home is heaven. "For we know that if the earthly tent which is our house is torn down, we have a building from God, a house not made with hands, eternal in the heavens" (2 Corinthians 4).

The Psalmist said, "Lord, remind me how brief my time on earth will be. Remind me that my days are numbered, and that my life is fleeing away" (Psalms 39:4).

Our present body is temporary and flimsy, frail, vulnerable, and wasting away. The things we see now are here today and gone tomorrow. The things we can't see now will last forever. By our participation in the resurrection of the life of Jesus (2 Corinthians 4:10) our mortal being is swallowed up by life, not by death.

Barbara Johnson is a woman well acquainted with losing children. She gives this wise counsel to parents of children who have taken their lives. "This is when you have to claim Deuteronomy 29:29, 'The secret things belong to the

Lord.' And this is a secret thing. No one will ever know the reason why this thing happened, this side of heaven. As I counsel many parents who have lost children to suicide, this is the hardest one to deal with. They want to blame themselves. I try to tell them that their child went out to meet a just and a loving God. And God only knows the answers. You can't blame yourself for what your kids do or grab onto guilt."

Bob and Karen realized they had been grieving over their son for more than thirty years. But, in time, they understood that out of God's providential, permissive will He allowed this suicide to take place. Satan had deceived David, to be sure, and they don't believe for a moment that God caused it. As I said at the beginning of this book, God is never the author of sin, but people's actions and intents are *used* by Him to serve His sovereign purpose (Romans 8:28).

Karen and Bob had prayed fervently for their son for years, but their prayers seemed unanswered as circumstances grew worse. But they were reminded by wise counsel that all prayers are not answered like we want them to be. God did answer their prayer. The moment David stepped into eternity, his life became perfect!

Someday, sooner than Karen and Bob think, there will be a wonderful reunion with David. It is not the kind we read about in the parable of the prodigal son. But just like the Father covered his son with his body to protect him, Jesus covered David's body with His body to save his soul. In the presence of our God and our king there will be a great celebration and much rejoicing. In the meantime, God has used Karen and Bob in the lives of hurting parents, to lend them hope and healing.

He wears a heavenly watch

I am learning that not all homecomings with a prodigal take place this side of eternity. The majority of them do, but not all. I hear many glorious stories of reconciliation, too numerous to write. But we must trust that God is at work *regardless* of the outcome this side of eternity. God wears a heavenly watch. If you leave the matter in His hands, you can trust Him to do what is right. God really does give you important answers, but often not the answers you were expecting. If you trust in Him, He will give you the answers you need. God gives you answers, and the greatest answer He ever gave is in His Son Jesus. It is when you have Jesus in your life that you are best equipped to find answers and to find the healing that you need.

We by our very nature are latched onto the temporal things of life. It's all we have experienced. It's hard to imagine that He really is working! Divine patience is to wait for God's promises. This involves being satisfied with God and God alone. It involves resting in the strength of God.

I pray that your prodigal comes home soon, but more importantly, I pray that regardless of the situation, you will allow Christ to be sufficient for every area of your life.

God's faithfulness

A few years ago I met a darling woman who shared her story of being a prodigal, and how God answered her mother's prayers.

"I grew up in what I refer to as the ideal home. My parents were full-time missionaries. They lived out their faith in their home and they walked the walk and talked the talk. Judy, I have nothing but praise for my parents.

"After I graduated from high school I decided to see what the world had to offer me. To sow some wild oats. I moved away from my folks, and began drinking, doing drugs, and living a promiscuous life. Finally I got pregnant and got married. I had a son, but the marriage was a disaster. Soon I filed for divorce. My life was now in a downward spiral.

"Every time I came home to visit my parents, I used all my 'God talk' with Mom and Dad. I thought I was the great imposter. I was sure Mom and Dad were buying into my double life.

"After one particular visit, Mom lovingly said, 'When are you going to stop playing all these games and get yourself right with the Lord?'

"'What? What do you mean? My life is great! I'm going to church and living for the Lord,' I snapped.

"But Mom knew the truth. She just continued to pray for me without ceasing.

"I continued my darkened lifestyle. I was a single mom, living a life of promiscuity and drugs.

"One day I got a dreaded phone call.

"'Mary, this is Dad. Your mom is very ill. You need to come home soon. She isn't going to last long.'

"I rushed to be by my mom's side, and she died within a few days. I grieved for months over losing my godly mother. I knew I'd never fooled her, and it was too late now to make things right.

"From a human viewpoint my mom's prayers were seemingly never answered. But I know now that was a lie. God was answering her prayers according to *His* timetable.

"Judy, a few years ago I came to the end of myself. I knew I was a phony. I cried out to God and told Him I wanted to leave my sinful life, and I asked Him to help me. I asked Him to forgive me, and I received Him as my Lord and Savior. Judy, *instantly* my life began to change. I do not have the time to tell you all that God has done for me and for my family. Amazingly the first change that came was a hunger for His Word. I became more aware of my sin than ever, and His precious grace and mercy that forgave me, and His offer for a new beginning. I cannot seem to get enough of Him, or serve Him enough. He's not only helped me get out of debt, He is putting back the pieces of my broken life. Judy, God is faithful. He answered my Mom's prayers, but it was fifteen years after she'd gone to heaven."

I think of this amazing verse:

"Suppose one of you had a hundred sheep and lost one. Wouldn't you leave the ninety-nine in the wilderness and go after the one until you found it? When found, you can be sure you would put it across your shoulders, rejoicing, and when you got home call in your friends and neighbors, saying 'Celebrate with me! I've found my lost sheep!' Count on it … there's more joy in heaven over one sinner's rescued life than over ninety-nine good people in no need of rescue" (Luke 15:4–7).

Jesus said, "My sheep hear my voice, and I know them and they follow me. I have given them eternal life and they shall never perish. No one shall snatch them away from me" (John 10:27–29).

God hears the cries of His children, He hears parents' prayers! He sees our life from the beginning into eternity. God is faithful! Nothing is impossible for Him!

I hope Mary's story is an encouragement to you to keep praying for your prodigal, and leave the timetable in God's hands.

He'll See Them Home

Don't despair so of your children,
God will bring them to the fold ....
Because He died to save them,
They're special to the Lord.
He knows how much you love them,
He loves them even more.
As long as you hold on in prayer,
He'll not close the door.
Even now He sees your tears,
And He whispers tenderly,
Of love that conquered all ...
That all men might be free.
So lay them at His altar,
Let go and leave them there ...
God will be faithful to your trust,
He won't withhold His care.
His hand will ever nurture,
No matter where they roam ...
And He won't be satisfied
'Til He sees them safely home!

—Joyce Henning

Steps to getting on with your life

* God's timetable is often quite different from ours.
* The Christian life is a walk of faith, not sight. When we put a timetable on our prayers, we have stopped walking by faith.
* God does not answer *all* prayers this side of eternity. We must have an eternal perspective. Remember Mary's mom, and *when* God answered her prayers?

* David's parents will see their son healed and whole in heaven.
* Keep in mind, this world is not our home.
* Wait patiently in great faith.
* God promises to go after His lost sheep. He'll lead them safely home.

"The center of God's will is our only safety."
—Betsy ten Boom

Chapter Eleven

Are You Ready to Live in Peace?

*"Peace is the deliberate adjustment of my life
to the will of God."*

—Anonymous

MARK, IN HIS late twenties, lived a vibrant and active life. He was tall, blond, tanned, good-looking, and admittedly pretty party-hardy most of his life. He said life was a blast and the future was as bright as the lights in a football stadium. "I love being in control of my life!"

Mark was a prodigal.

Like most people Mark wasn't counting on any adversity in his life, much less suffering. In his late twenties, work, alcohol, drugs, and living for self was his routine.

Suddenly he began developing physical symptoms that he knew were not normal. He experienced unexplained stumbling. He'd fall down for no apparent reason. A slight weakness developed, first in his hand, then his foot. He ignored them, but they persisted.

After brooding over the possibilities, Mark reluctantly made an appointment with a doctor. His heart was pounding as he dialed the phone.

The doctor ordered a battery of tests. Waiting for the results was agony. But the dreaded phone call came. The shocking verdict was in; Lou Gehrig's Disease.

Mark's heart skipped several beats. His mind was a quagmire of thoughts.

"This disease is a progressive neurological illness, and there is no known cure. Unfortunately the disease is fatal, and can often advance quite rapidly," the doctor explained in a somber voice.

Mark sat in deafening silence, like a marionette whose strings had been cut.

Mark couldn't believe it! He got a second opinion. But the diagnosis was the same. Mark went into denial, refusing to accept the diagnosis.

The symptoms increased, and even picked up speed.

A former drinking buddy had recently come to faith in Jesus Christ. He shared the gospel with Mark. God had been wooing Mark and preparing him to hear the Good News. That day Mark received Him as his Lord and Savior.

Mark began going to church. He devoured the Word of God. He couldn't get enough of this new banquet cuisine. The more he ate the hungrier his appetite for spiritual truth grew.

Mark's health declined at warp speed. He was forced to cut back at work, and finally he reluctantly resigned. The medical bills were met by his insurance company but the disability checks afforded Mark little income. The same friend who'd introduced him to Christ began taking care of

Mark physically and financially. He hired help to come in when he couldn't be there and cared for him in the evenings. He took Mark to church every weekend, and Bible study on Tuesday mornings.

The men in his Bible study wrapped their hearts and their lives around Mark. They tangibly shared his burdens.

The Word of God was having a powerful effect on Mark's life. God was transforming him and providing him with the grace to go through these uncharted waters.

In the fall he went to the men's retreat in a special wheelchair. He just loved being there. He made every effort to sing the praise songs, but he was unable to use his arms any longer. Someone noticed him weeping during the praise session.

"What's wrong? Is there something I can do to help ya', Buddy?"

"Oh, no, I'm okay! I just miss raising my arms and praising my wonderful Savior."

From that point on, every time a praise song was sung, the men on either side of Mark held up his arms. It was a precious and emotional sight to see the Body of Christ become his arms!

Right in the midst of these incredibly difficult circumstances, in a body weakened and racked with disease, something wonderful happened.

Mark laid his life before the Father.

"Lord, I surrender my entire life and agenda over to you today. One-hundred percent, Lord. I choose to let You have Your way. Thank you for allowing this so I would hear Your voice and receive You as my Savior. Thank You, that I can share my story with others. Use me, Lord, to bring glory to You."

In this place of agony, Mark discovered the abundant Christian life Jesus promised. God lavished Mark with total, unexplainable peace. Peace that is a supernatural gift provided by the Holy Spirit of God in a heart that has finally given up throne rights.

Mark learned what many of us miss: God alone is everything we need! His life-giving words and His presence satisfy *permanently*. Mark realized that living in *His* care is the only hope for satisfaction and real life. Mark didn't look back and long for the olden days of prestige, partying, prosperity, and a perfect body. He was experiencing what Paul reveled in, the fellowship of His suffering. Christ is nearest to His suffering children. Mark experienced the reality of the Christian life, peace in the midst of pain!

One day a physical therapist came to his apartment to help with his therapy. He'd been there so many times. He was intrigued with Mark's contentment.

"Hey, Buddy, I just have to ask you a couple of questions. How in the world do you live with this? I can't figure you out. You've basically lost your life. You've lost your job, your freedom, your health, and almost all mobility. And yet you aren't angry or bitter. In fact, you seem really happy. You blow me away! What's up?"

Mark's speech was much slower now, and he found it almost agonizing to articulate his words, but he began to explain the secret of his contentment.

"Joe, this is the greatest time in my life. Because, you see, I have learned the secret to life. Jesus is all you need. I have been blind most of my life, but now I see clearly. Happiness depends on circumstances. But joy and peace come from God alone. I praise Him for allowing me to experience this. I have the kind of joy one only dreams about! It's all from my Heavenly Father. My mind is fixed upon Him. He saved me from my sins, gave me a purpose for living, and He's providing a place for me in heaven. I may be a prisoner of my body right now, but I have freedom I've never known. I give Him all the praise and glory!"

God squeezed a timeless message from Mark, and shined the spotlight on his response to this trial. It spoke deeply to a physical therapist and did bring God glory.

Two months later Mark went home to be with His Lord and His King.

Miracles still happen

As parents with a prodigal child, initially we are all paralyzed with grief. We can't believe it's happening to us. We don't want anyone to know. But in time, we come to grips with it. We start sharing our pain with dear friends. We start dealing with things. But until we come to the end of ourselves, and give everything to God, we will not be able to get on with our lives.

This miracle was available to Abraham when he was asked to sacrifice his only son, Isaac, on the altar. But God provided a ram just in time.

Imagine offering to sacrifice your prodigal on an altar. Imagine trusting God in such a deep, unthinkable way. But because of Christ, we don't have to offer a sacrificial lamb anymore. The Lamb of God paid the final sacrifice. "He who did not spare His own Son, but delivered Him over for us all, how will he not also with Him freely give us all things?" (Romans 8:32 NASB).

God wants to freely give us *all* things. What are all things? Spiritual transformation that sets us free!

"As long as we are fighting God for control, we will be the one that loses," says A. W. Tozer. "The reason why many Christians are still troubled, still seeking, still making little forward progress, is because they haven't yet come to the end of themselves. They are still trying to give orders, and interfering with God's work within us."

God was patiently waiting for my husband and me to come to the end of ourselves so He could set us free. It happened on a Christmas Eve. We were all alone. Our hearts were heavy. The heartbreak of our family breakdown closed in on us. With less than spirited holiday fervor, we unwrapped our gifts out of listless duty. The gifts meant absolutely nothing.

Suddenly my husband stopped opening his presents and said, "I think we should pray!" I thought he'd lost his mind. Pray? While unwrapping presents? "Do we need prayer for that?" I reasoned in my usual sarcastic mode. I said nothing, but I got down on my knees, and immediately began to cry. I began to weep uncontrollably. I wailed out loud, "Help us, God!"

Obviously I cannot recall every single word my husband prayed, but it was something like this:

"God, we have come to the end of ourselves. We can't go on anymore. We are worn out. First, we want to thank You for allowing this pain in our lives, but often it's so deep. We will never give up on You, God, but we need Your help. We can't change these circumstances, but You can. Lord, tonight we give our child to You. We know we can trust You to take this mess and work it all out. We know You know all our needs. God, give us back our joy. The joy of our salvation."

"Lord," I added, "thank you for the amazing way you've walked through this pain with us. There are days I feel your presence in such tangible ways, and other days I feel I haven't learned a thing and the pain is new and fresh. God, I know You love us more than we love our child. Do whatever it takes to bring change to us and to our prodigal. Amen."

That starry Christmas night our hearts were submissive, and surrendered.

What happened next was the miracle. We were *flooded* with peace. Amazing peace. Peace in the midst of pain! God's transforming power *in* us that brings change. The greatest gift, Christmas or otherwise, a person can receive!

The reality of Christ's words in John 14:27 made sense to me for the first time in my life. "My peace I leave with you; my peace I give to you; not as the world gives do I give to you. Do not let your heart be troubled, nor let it be fearful."

Then another verse seemed to pop into my mind: "I [Jesus] have told you these things, so that in me you may have peace. In this world you will have trouble. But take heart! I have overcome the world" (John 16:33).

The Greek for the meaning of "overcome the world" is *nikao*, which means to conquer, prevail, and to carry off the victory. For the Christian this means we can be confident in *Him* so we can hold fast to our faith unto death against the powers of the evil one, our foes, temptations, and persecutions.

All true peace is from Jesus Christ. This world cannot offer us lasting peace. But God wants *all* His children to come to this place of surrender to receive it. Not just parents of prodigals. His Word says He will withhold no good thing from those who walk uprightly (Psalms 84:11b). The phenomenal result of worshiping God and submitting to

His Lordship is that you experience peace in your heart, a peace that goes deeper than the circumstances around you.

As I said at the beginning of this book, often we are convinced we will die if we have to live without someone, especially one of our children. But imagine for a moment experiencing this supernatural peace and grace to live a fruitful life if nothing *ever* changes in your life. This is the Christ-life we're all searching for. He is the Prince of Peace. If there is reconciliation down the road, hallelujah. But while you wait, you can live in peace.

I am learning, day by day, that Jesus Christ is sufficient to provide His children with everything they need for life! Peter said, "His divine power has granted us everything pertaining to life and godliness, through the true knowledge of Him who called us by His own glory and excellence" (2 Peter 1:3). He's the only one who can. He wants to *be* our life. All the rest is just surplus! Overflow! *Real* living comes only from Christ.

We need to be reminded daily that doing the Father's will does *not* guarantee a painless life! Jesus never did anything *but* the Father's will, and He suffered and died for it! Every disciple suffered greatly as he healed people and brought them the Good News. All died violent deaths.

Yet His power unmistakably present in our lives in *unthinkable* circumstances is the secret to *really* living.

Parent, do you want that power? Do you want to have that kind of peace? Freedom to get on with life?

Jesus Christ, God's supreme gift to save us, will freely provide whatever we need to live in peace. But remember there *is* a condition. We must first trust the Most High God enough to be able to lay our agenda down for *His*.

Wayne Barber put it this way: "The Christian life is not a matter of getting anything. It's about entering into what we already have *in* Christ. Only by being connected with Christ through faith can anyone enter into eternal life and only through a continuing connection with Him can we have this power for a life filled with peace."

How is this supernatural power transferred or accomplished in our lives? We must let go of our old ways of acting. We must be *transformed!* It's a metamorphosis that comes from the Holy Spirit of God in our heart. Matthew uses the same word, *transformed*, to describe the Transfiguration in Matt. 17:2. Just as Christ briefly and in a limited way displayed outwardly His inner, divine nature and glory at the Transfiguration, we as His children have available to us this same transforming power as the Holy Spirit changes our thinking.

Ian Thomas put it another way: "We need to come to our wits' end because *then* we are ready to say: 'God, I can't!' Then God says back to us, "I know, I never said you could, but I can, and I always said I would ... do it through you."

When you get to your wits' end, you'll find God lives there.

Steps to getting on with your life

* Peace is through Christ *alone.*
* God wants you to receive His transforming power to experience peace.
* Parent, have you come to your wits' end?
* Today is the day to lay your agenda down for God's plan.

❊ Tell Him, "Lord, I give up! I cannot go on any longer. I need Your power to do this. I want to live a surrendered life, centered on Your will. I'm through giving You orders. I give you my child today and I take my hands off this situation and give it to You. Give me Your peace, the gift You promised. Thank you, in Jesus' name, amen."

❊ Parent, make surrender a lifestyle.

"Peace rules the day when Christ rules the mind."
—Anonymous

Chapter Twelve

Getting On With Your Life

"All heaven is waiting to help those who will
discover the will of God and do it."
—J. Robert Ashcroft

WHEN MY PHONE rang several years ago, I had no idea God
was going to use our pain to help someone else.

"Judy, my name is Kathy. I am a friend of Janice," she
said in a very whispery, lovely tone of voice.

"I am so glad you called."

As our phone conversation began Kathy laid out ten
years of devastation and pain they'd gone through with
their son Lance.

"He was a happy youngster, and we raised him in a
Christian home. He was active in youth groups and made a
decision to receive Christ at a youth camp. We had a very
strong family life, and we tried to live out our faith in front
of our children. We took them camping, taught them how
to fish and hunt. We provided many delightful memories
for them."

She admitted they'd made their mistakes, but they
adored their children, were very involved in their lives, dis-

ciplined out of love, set boundaries and curfews, and provided a secure life. She told me her son had a very strong relationship with his dad.

"We've never been people that drink alcohol or smoke. We tried to set the best example.

"But during high school the father of one of Lance's baseball teammates told us Lance was smoking pot. We nearly dropped over, we were so shocked! 'Not our son!' we protested.

"We confronted Lance immediately. He became very defensive at our accusations! 'Hey, I am a Christian and I would never drink or use drugs!'

"We chose to believe him.

"After Lance graduated from high school, he went out of state to college on a baseball scholarship, but soon dropped out and moved home. He started going to a local college, and moved into his own apartment. But he seemed to be depressed most of the time. He couldn't stick with anything. He lacked direction. Things just weren't adding up! There was always chaos. Car accidents, speeding tickets, late nights, unpaid bills, and empty pockets! His life was out of control. We sent him to a counselor who told us he had a personality disorder, and a chemical imbalance. The counselor suggested medication."

I listened to the all-too-familiar story of a prodigal child and a parent in excruciating pain, trying to make sense of it all.

"Kathy, I believe you need to face up to these red flags! There is a good chance your son is still using drugs."

Kathy later admitted that as I was telling her this, her stomach did flip-flops and she went into brain freeze. She felt like the air had been sucked out of her lungs, too!

These were not the words she wanted to hear. Surely I was wrong. She was hoping our phone call could provide a formula for fixing her son.

I began sharing a bit of our story of pain and disappointment.

"Kathy, I've learned that the circumstances you are going through are for a reason. God is either going to use you to be His ambassador to a darkened world, or He's going to reveal some areas in your own life that are not yet conformed into the image of His son. He does this through our circumstances, because we live in difficult ones almost every day. I want to assure you of one thing! God *is* in control, and no matter how bleak things appear, He wants to show you what an incredible God He is. We often think our trials are all about us. But the truth is, they are all about God and what He wants to do in and through us. But there is something you must do before He can help you."

"What, tell me?" she said in a pensive voice.

"Kathy, you need to give your son to the Lord. You need to lay him at the foot of the cross, and let him go. You must do this, or you will live in utter devastation and fear until God changes his life. There is nothing you can do to change him. You've tried everything. I can assure you this surrender will not be a one-time thing … but each day … you must give Him to God. Then saturate yourself in His Word, pray His promises daily, and gather around you some dear friends to pray for you and your son and help you stay focused on the Lord. Allow God to supernaturally comfort you and develop a deeper level of intimacy with Him. There'll come a day when He floods you with His supernatural peace because He has *become* your life."

"Oh, I am so frightened, Judy. What if something happens to our son?" she cried out.

"You know, it *is* frightening. It could be the biggest test of your life. But God is asking you to trust Him. To walk by faith, not sight. God gave you your son. He created him. But He didn't give him to you to be your reason for living. Kathy, I can assure you of this; it's impossible to let our children go in our own power. Ask Him to give you His power and peace to trust Him with everything! I am learning that I cannot trust my feelings; I can only tell you what God says in His Word. He is faithful."

Then I went into more detail about our entire journey with our prodigal. I wanted her to know the years we had lived in heartache. Then I was able to tell her of God's miraculous work in our lives, and how He'd changed us. For the first time in our conversation, I heard some hope in her voice!

"Oh, I pray that happens."

"I know it will," I assured her.

You see, Kathy's circumstances had so consumed her, she was spiraling into an abyss and Satan was rubbing his hands together with glee. He had attacked her mind, unleashed his assaults on her emotions, and she'd lost all hope. But Kathy, like all hurting parents, needed a new perspective. A perspective from God's Word. Kathy needed to arm herself with those weapons of mass destruction with which to fight off the fiery darts of the evil one.

"Kathy, as you begin to face the truth, and *stop* trying to rescue him, he will have to come to the end of himself in order to see his need to repent. That doesn't mean you stop loving him, but stop bailing him out of all his messes. Let sin run its course. The longer you reward his behavior, the harder his heart will grow, and the more you prolong the inevitable. Lance is in the pigpen, and God wants its power to be unleashed so it can do its work."

"The pigpen?" she cried out.

"Yep … that's what it is!" I said as lovingly as I could. "But promise me you won't lose hope. God is sufficient for getting His children out of pigpens. You are in a huge spiritual battle right now, and God wants to fight it for you."

We continued exchanging stories and prayed together, and said our good-byes. Little did I know it would be the beginning of one of the sweetest friendships I've ever known.

Bending the knee

Kathy told me in our next phone call that after she'd hung up the phone she and her husband admitted they felt like two ostriches. They'd buried their heads in the sands of denial for ten years hoping problems would simply go away. Oh, how I could relate. It's hard to face the pain. But until we know what we're facing, how will we know how to pray?

She went on to tell me, "At midnight, my husband and I knelt before our fireplace, and we envisioned the cross. We cried out to God for mercy. 'Lord, have mercy on Lance! Have mercy on us, too. Father, thank you for giving us this precious child, your gift to us. Thank you for giving us hope again. Thank you that we can put our faith and our trust in You and let You handle things now. You love Lance much more than we ever could. Please forgive us for our sin of unbelief, not believing You are in control of our circumstances, and our lives. Father, have your way in our lives and give us your peace. Thank you for orchestrating these circumstances for us to connect with a family halfway across the country to give us some encouragement and remind us of your power and your sufficiency. We pray this in Jesus' name."

When she and her husband got up off their knees, they had a renewed sense of hope.

Kathy's son was twenty-six at the time she called me. Over the next few years they would experience deep, dark valleys and then inch toward hope. They had some days when they thought God had forsaken them, but the more they stayed in God's Word, and prayed about everything, the stronger their faith grew. They began trusting God instead of their feelings.

Soon I got a computer and we began e-mailing each other daily. Some days I could tell it was all Kathy could do to keep from giving up hope, but there was definite change. Kathy had a lot of friends in her life, but none that had experienced the pain of living with a child who had broken their heart.

Coming to wit's end

She said there were days she would be so blue, and then check her e-mail, and I'd sent her something that encouraged her heart. This was the Holy Spirit prompting me to encourage a sister-in-Christ! "Rejoice with those who rejoice; mourn with those who mourn" (Romans 12:15).

It became increasingly difficult for Kathy and her husband to relate to their son, knowing the truth about his lifestyle. Kathy said she didn't know how to be a mom anymore. "I don't know if he comes around infrequently just to get something from us, or if he misses us and wants to be part of our family," she'd cry.

Her struggles were so much like ours. On one hand God tells us to love others unconditionally, but sometimes we must step away and love them from a distance.

"When Lance is around, there is such tension, and he's just not himself. He's very quiet, and preoccupied. I know he's living a double life."

Soon their son became a stranger to them. He was just a shell of a man. There would be long periods of time they didn't hear from him. Like most moms, Kathy worried her son was ill, hurt, or might not still be alive.

But one day Kathy came to her wits' end. She couldn't go on with this gripping pain. She cried out to God and released her son. It just happened! What followed was this inexplicable peace that came over her. She e-mailed me.

"Judy, Judy, it happened! Today, I was set free. I am free from this incredible bondage of agony, fear, and torment. Judy, Jesus has given me peace! I can't explain it!"

A few months later she shared their secret heartache with their couples' Bible study. They asked them to pray. It was a huge step for them because they were so embarrassed by their son, and didn't want anyone to know about his life. But that night a group of wonderful prayer warriors began seeking the Throne of God on behalf of Lance.

Coming home

In the parable of the prodigal son, we read, "When he was a long way off, his father saw him. His heart pounding, he ran out, embraced him, and kissed him. The son started his speech, 'Father I've sinned against God, I've sinned before you; I don't deserve to be called your son ever again.' But the father said to his servants, 'Quickly bring out the best robe and put it on him, and put a ring on his hands and sandals on his feet. Then get a grain-fed heifer and roast it. We're going to feast! We're going to have a wonderful time! My son is here ... given up for dead and now alive! Given up for lost and now found!' And they began to have a wonderful time" (Luke 15:21–25).

(Note that Old Testament law required rebellious children to be stoned to death. The father knew the townspeople were watching, and he wanted to protect his son from imminent death. It is a beautiful picture of how Jesus covers our body with His to save us from death and eternal separation from a Holy God.)

The next month after Kathy's admission to the prayer group, the tragic events of 9/11 happened. Lance was at his apartment watching all the coverage on TV. It shook his emotions badly. He looked at the filth he'd been living in, the brevity of life, the wasted years, the sin in the pigpen, his empty, meaningless existence. A few nights later, as he lay in bed, he began to weep over his sins. He fell to his knees on his bedroom floor and began to wail. He crawled out to his tiny living room, rolled over, and wept for hours. Exhausted, spent, he wanted to get up and go to bed, but he physically couldn't. Like Jacob, Lance was wrestling with God. He sobbed on the floor for the entire night and finally, in the morning, he came to his senses, and he surrendered his life to Christ.

Kathy and her husband were up at their cabin that weekend. Lance's car was not running, so he managed to rent one. Determined to share what had happened with his parents, he drove seven hours to their cabin. As he started down the long dirt driveway to the cabin, he thought of his mom and his dad, and all the heartache he'd caused them.

He stopped his car about a hundred feet from the cabin, got out and started walking down that dusty road to their front door. About halfway there, he looked up, and his mom and dad were walking to meet him. The three of them embraced and wept as he told them he'd come home to the Lord. She said it was the greatest day of their lives. God had changed him totally. He was repentant, kind, and filled with humility and love. "I say to you that likewise there will be more joy in heaven over one sinner who repents than over ninety-nine just persons who need no repentance" (Luke 15:7).

Today Lance has a new life. He's working at a job that has great potential and a future. He's in a Bible study and never misses church. He's hoping God will bring along someone to share his life with someday. In the meantime, he's living one day at a time. He is also in a recovery/support program.

Kathy would admit that this trial changed her and her husband *spiritually* more than anything else they ever lived through. It matured their walk with Christ. They learned His sufficiency in all circumstances.

The trials of life that distress us all can eventually produce in us the super-joy of going clear through them. These very things—tribulation, distress, persecution, and pain—produce in us this joy. They are not things to fight. We are more than conquerors through Him in all things, not in spite of them, but in the midst of them.

I find that God seldom allows me to choose the way He will use pain in my life. But often it is pain that becomes a platform for ministering to other people who are experiencing the same pain we've gone through.

"Praise be to the God and Father of our Lord Jesus Christ, the Father of compassion and the God of all comfort, who comforts us in all our troubles, so that we can comfort those in any trouble with the comfort we ourselves have received from God" (2 Corinthians 1:3–4).

Every trial we have endured with our prodigal child has been used to comfort other parents who are suffering. My prayer is that you will help other parents get on with their lives.

In the second chapter of this book, I told the story of my friend Debbie, and how ill prepared I was to lend her any hope.

But down the road Debbie got serious about her walk with Christ, too, and became passionate about His Word and the power of prayer. Her walk with Christ today is rock-solid. She lives in peace and joy.

Has her daughter left the pigpen? Sadly, not yet! But there came a day when they simply gave her to God, and let her go into His capable hands. They have not given up, but instead pray with great faith. They are soaring above their circumstances. They are living in peace. Peace that God gives to parents of prodigals, so they can get on with their lives.

Epilogue

WE'VE COME TO the end of the book. I hope you have been encouraged by other people's stories, encouraged by God and His Word, given renewed hope, peace, and purpose for the future.

If you are still in the "waiting room," I know you long for your prodigal to return. You agonize daily about it, but hopefully you realize that God has allowed this incredible adversity to change you and allow you to experience His sufficiency in all things. Each day you pray, He reminds you that the timetable for homecomings belongs to Him. I think it's important to remember that God loves your prodigal more than you do. He's at work.

Next, I believe one of the greatest things you can do until that homecoming day is to live the most godly, wonderful, exciting, joy-filled, abundant Christian life as evidence of your relationship with Christ. Your life can testify to the fact that there is no happier life, no more fulfilling life than the one found in abiding with Jesus daily. In time your prodigal will see that in you.

The hope in the parable of the prodigal is that he did come to his senses. He knew he could go home again.

That's important. When he did go home, the father ran to meet him. He met him halfway. He displayed affection.

I have given so much thought to our prodigal. Would I rather have had a docile, passive child who was always obedient? A child who never pushed the envelope, or stepped out of the boundaries, yet never really followed Christ with any passion?

Or would I rather have had a child we raised in the way of the Lord and went on a rebellious journey, wallowed in the pigpen, maybe more than once, genuinely repented and came back to the Lord? Some days I think the passive child might have made our lives easier. But long term, I wonder if I would have ever discovered what Paul called the Christ life? Would we have the confidence and the peace of the Lord had we not gone through suffering? Out of our suffering emerged two stronger souls. Our hearts have been seared, but I believe our character has been changed. Would we ever have had such keen hearing to His call had our hearts not been broken? Would our marriage be as rock-solid if we hadn't experienced this time of agony and learned to cling tightly to each other daily?

I confess I wouldn't trade a minute of what we have been through. God has changed us. He's still changing us. But we will not be complete until we stand in His presence.

Jesus said, "Anyone who intends to come with me has to let me lead. You're not in the driver's seat ... I am. Don't run from suffering, embrace it. Follow me and I'll show you how. Self-help is no help at all. Self-sacrifice is the way, my way, to finding yourself, your true self. What good would it do to get everything you want and lose you, the real you?" (Luke 9:23, *The Message*)

We've been through the fire, and God has refined us. But we know there will be more fires up ahead until we reach our eternal home. His supernatural grace and peace will carry us.

In the meantime, parent, I encourage you to keep praying. God is at work!

Works Cited

Scriptures used throughout the book are New International Version, New American Standard Bible, *The Message*, and *The Living Bible*.

Chapter One
Anderson, Neil. *Freedom from Addiction*. Regal Books, 1996.

Bradenton, Ann W. Christian *Parenting Today*. January/February 2000.

Chapter Two
Bridges, Jerry. *Trusting God Even When Life Hurts*. NavPress, 1998.

Chapter Three
Stowell, Joseph (president of Moody Bible Institute). Quoted from daily devotional Griefshare.com.

Chapter Four
Anderson, Neil. *Bondage Breaker*. Harvest House Publishers, 1993.

Wiersbe, Warren. *The Strategy of Satan: How to Detect and Defeat Him.* Wheaton, Illinois: Tyndale House Publishers, Inc., 1987.

Chapter Five
Waldrep, Phil. *Parenting Prodigals.* Baker Press, 2001.

Chapter Six
Anderson, Neil. *Bondage Breaker.* Harvest House Publishers, 1993.

Chapter Seven
Arthur, Kay. *As Silver Refined.* Waterbrook Press, 1997.

Johnson, Barbara. *Splashes of Joy in the Cesspools of Life.* Word Publishing (quote from Griefshare.com).

One-Year-Bible. Tyndale House.

Warren, Rick. *The Purpose Driven Life.* Zondervan, 2002.

Verses on the sovereignty of God: Ez. 6:14; Job 37:23, 38:1–4; Rev. 19:6; I Cor. 2:9–12; I Tim. 6:15; Acts 17:24–28; Ps. 31:15, 9:10; Matt. 10:29; Lam. 3:37–38; Rom. 11:33; Deut. 4:39; Judges 14:1–4; II Chron. 20:6; Prov. 21:1; Ps. 47:1–3; Job 9:12, 22:12, 41:11; Ps. 8:1, 9:7–8, 135:6, 29:10, 139:5–12, 83:18; Prov. 16:9, 20:24; Ecc. 3:14; Is. 14:24, 25:1, 37:26, 43:13; Deut. 32:39; Is. 44:24–25, 45:5–6, 43:10; Rev. 1:17; 2:8, 22:13; Daniel 4:34–37; John 19:11; Rom. 9:14–24; Col. 1:15–20; I Tim. 1:17; Rev. 1:15, 3:7–8, 17:14, 22:13.

Chapter Eight
Arthur, Kay. *Spiritual Warfare Devotional.*

Cymbala, Jim. *Fresh Wind, Fresh Fire.* Zondervan, 1997.

Moore, Beth. *Praying God's Word.* Broadman & Holdman.

Chapter Nine
Allendar, Dan. *Bold Love.*

Kendall, R. T. *Total Forgiveness.*

Lucado, Max. *When God Whispers Your Name.*

Swindoll, Chuck. *Growing Strong in the Seasons of Life.*

Chapter Ten
Johnson, Barbara. *Splashes of Joy in the Cesspool of Life.*
Word Publishing (quotes from Griefshare.com).

Chapter Eleven
Thomas, Ian. *The Saving Life of Christ.*

About the Author

POPULAR INTERNATIONAL SPEAKER Judy Hampton is best known for being transparent, authentic, extremely humorous, and biblical. Her testimony has aired on the *Focus on the Family* radio broadcast, *The Billy Graham Association's Decision Today*, and *Moody Radio*. She has also appeared on several television programs, including *At Home Live With Chuck and Jenni* and *Insight: Television for Women*, and teaches two sessions on DVD for the CBA Silver Medallion Award-winning series *Doing Life Together* (Rick Warren's Purpose Driven Group Resources).

Judy's freelance articles have been published in several magazines. She is a contributing author of more than twenty-five books, including *Chicken Soup for the Christian Woman's Soul* and the *Kisses of Sunshine* series (for Women and Grandmas). Her first book, *Under The Circumstances*, is also an eleven-week Bible study.

Contact information
E-mail: jhampton60@aol.com
www.judyhampton.com

Printed in the United States
200090BV00002B/106-210/A

9 781587 364723